TEMPUS
Oral History
SERIES

YORK
voices

Arthur and Eve Briggs behind the bar at the Bay Horse, Marygate in the 1950s.

TEMPUS
Oral History
SERIES

YORK

voices

Compiled by
Van Wilson

TEMPUS

First published 1999
Copyright © Van Wilson, 1999

Tempus Publishing Limited
The Mill, Brimscombe Port,
Stroud, Gloucestershire, GL5 2QG

ISBN 0 7524 1680 4

Typesetting and origination by
Tempus Publishing Limited
Printed in Great Britain by
Midway Clark Printing, Wiltshire

To my brothers and sister-in-law – Michael and Gill May, and Richard Potter.

ROWNTREE MEMORIAL PARK, YORK

Rowntree Park with lake, in the 1920s.

CONTENTS

ACKNOWLEDGEMENTS

I would like to thank the following people who have been very helpful in the process of compiling this book:

York Oral History Society for the use of photographs and material from their archives; The staff of York City Archives; David Poole for assistance with locating names and places; Tricia Scott for interviewing and transcribing Mrs Ann Harding's story; and especially Mike Race for assisting me with interviews and collecting photographs, and for reading the manuscript, offering constructive criticism and making useful comments.

I wish to thank all those who generously shared both their stories and photographs with myself and the York society. This book is a tribute to them all.

INTRODUCTION

As we approach the Millennium, there is a growing desire to look back and view with nostalgia the last 100 years. There are many things which have changed over the last century – education, the workplace, attitudes towards women, as well as the way we spend our leisure time. The advent of the technological age has opened doors of opportunity. Medicine has improved the quality of life and increased our longevity but the stresses and strains of modern living 'in the fast lane' still take their toll. Labour-saving machinery has afforded us more free time but some might say that this has led to a rise in crime. There have been huge advances in transport and communication. In the pre-First World War era, the world seemed an enormous place and opportunities to travel to other continents were rare. Today, travel over thousands of miles is usual and the World Wide Web offers the chance to communicate with people anywhere in the world in minutes. Our ancestors may find today's society too liberal and less disciplined, being used to a quieter, perhaps saner, kind of life, whereas young people today may regard their forebears as old-fashioned and their lifestyles rather primitive. There is something to be said for both viewpoints.

Many books have been written about the history of York through different eras and some of the more recent publications on the city feature an element of oral history. Oral history is not, of course, a new phenomenon. It is as old as the human race itself. But the translation of oral testimony into the written form is relatively new. Diaries and collections of letters are useful in telling us something of the lives of our ancestors but they tend to be selective in content. Oral history in its original form, as spoken history, is valuable because it is real and alive, giving us information about ordinary, everyday life which is normally missing from history textbooks. The oral historian is privileged to be able to share in this very personal form of history. There is much we can learn, in this way, from those who have lived before us.

The York Oral History Society was founded in 1982 and has been collecting and preserving the stories of people in the city since that time; and is committed to handing those stories back to the community in the form of books, plays and exhibitions. This volume is the first general oral history of York, capturing voices of the twentieth century that have not been heard before, together with contemporary photographs appearing for the first time in any publication. In the course of seeking out stories and selecting subjects to share their perspectives on life in York, I wanted to find people who could talk about a way of life which has largely disappeared.

I have combined a number of recent interviews of my own with interviews conducted by York Oral History Society over the last few years. The result is a mixture of stories featuring men and women from different walks of life – sharing their memories of childhood, young adulthood, work, play, sport, church, wartime and transport – covering the whole spectrum of life.

As the twenty-first century approaches, it has been fascinating to compare the experiences of those who lived in the early part of the twentieth century with our way of life today. In the last section of this book, I examine the life of a York girl living in 1900, and that of her great-grandson living in 1999. Between them lies a century of change, a century which has probably seen the greatest changes of any such period in the history of the world. The child of 1900 would never in her wildest dreams have imagined the life that we know in the year 1999. The child of 1999, more accustomed to the advances in technology and the prevalence of science fiction, finds it far easier to imagine what life will be like in 2100.

A comprehensive look at the voices of our century should include those of all classes, if it claims to represent the whole strata of society. In the late twentieth century, classes are not so easy to define, and the boundaries are blurred. The old county families have largely dispersed, the middle classes have expanded and overtaken the working class in numbers, as education at a higher level has become much more commonplace than it was, even up until the Second World War. Today's university student would perhaps have been yesterday's errand boy or kitchen maid. Society has progressed and the opportunities for improvement and education are now available to almost all. This change has brought about many differences in both our way of life and our thinking, but the experiences of our parents and grandparents should not be forgotten, as they forged the path which led to our present way of life. The voices in this book are a representation of 'York voices' – they vary from nursemaids and farm servants to international authors, sportsmen, councillors and engineers. I believe that each of them has something to say which is worth hearing.

Van Wilson
July 1999

CHAPTER 1
Childhood and family

Tang Hall Bridge, which separates Tang Hall from Heworth, 1910.

Station Hotel on the right of York station, 1920s.

In the days before 'bedroom culture', in which television, videos and computer games are an 'essential' part of a child's life, children spent much more time playing outside. Hilda Beaumont lived in Heworth, now a suburb of York, which in her youth was still countryside.

A Child's Eye View

It's all bungalows now. There's a bridge and the stream is still there where we could see kingfishers. When I was at Queen Anne's, the botany mistress asked us to pick all the flowers we could find. Everybody else had about six, but Phil and I didn't go anywhere except our hayfield and we got over eighty different flowers. All along the hedge bottom we looked for celandines and violets in springtime. One of the best things I remember with pleasure, was being waked up every morning in the summer with the dawn chorus. About five o'clock in the morning they would start and again in the evening. There was a very tall poplar and a thrush used to go to the top every night and absolutely pour it out. It was lovely.

Hilda Beaumont, born 1904

Sunday Treat

We used to have a walk on a Sunday in the brickyard. We'd go over a wooden bridge on Leeman Road, just a narrow cinder path where the trains pass underneath. My grandmother lived up Carr Lane and we'd go and see her. That was our treat. The whole family went – eleven for home-made raspberry jam and bread. We were happy, happy as bees.

There wasn't no radios, we used to sing. And during the war we sang a hymn every Sunday night for everybody we knew – and one for my brother. He was a page boy at the Station Hotel and then he went into the Navy, on a merchant ship from Liverpool to Canada throughout the First World War, but he came back all right.

Margaret Brown, born 1900

Grandma's Grocery

My great-grandmother was born in 1844, she had a large family. I think there were seven children and most of them lived in York and we were very close and used to do a great deal of socialising, with lovely parties at Uncle Tom's at Christmas time. I always remember they had a huge rabbit pie in a big enamel bowl because there were about twenty of us. And they had a concert party. One of the family, Lenny, was on the music halls and he played with Charlie Chaplin and was quite a good comedian. Grandmother was married and had four children but her husband went off to America to seek his fortune and he was going to send for grandma, but he never came back again and my uncle Dick said he was drowned in a steamer coming back to England. So grandma had a very rough time with four children to bring up and she opened little shops. She had one on Acomb Road but the one I remember was opposite St Mary Bishophill Junior church.

She sold more or less everything. It was the only grocer's shop there and she had a big wooden flour bin. Flour didn't come in three pound bags like it does now. It came in sacks and you'd go and buy a stone at a time. The sugar came loose and it was always put in blue bags. She'd get up early in the morning and bake because opposite was a factory and all the men called at grandma's to buy fresh breadcakes.

She married again, a blind man who was a very good pianist. He played at the Fishergate Picture Palace and being blind he couldn't see the pictures but my aunt Lily used to sit beside him and she would whisper 'cowboys' and he would play the appropriate music and hearts and flowers for love scenes and such as that. We used to go to the Grand picture house on a Saturday afternoon and it was tuppence or threepence and they had serials on and you knew that the heroine would be tied to a railway line at the end and you had to wait until next week to see what happened. I believe one of the famous stars at that time was Pearl White.

My own father was blind too, he went blind with measles when he was seven and he came to the Yorkshire School for the Blind. It was a very tough life. In wintertime they had to break the ice to get washed. Eventually he worked there and became a very good basket-maker. In fact he was so good that they sent him off to exhibitions such as the Yorkshire Show to demonstrate. He was surprisingly well educated even though

Yorkshire School for the Blind, 1929.

he was blind because he was a proficient Braille reader. He wanted me to try and learn, but I don't think my fingers were delicate enough. My mother was marvellous, she'd read books to him and she said that she learned a lot being married to him. My father taught her a lot and she became a good reader and read all the classical things.

We had a family doctor called Dr Craig and when my mother was ill in 1921 and needed an operation, he did the operation free but my father had to find the money for hospital treatment. It was an urgent operation and she had to go to the Purey Cust nursing home and I think dad borrowed the money. Dr Craig was a marvellous doctor, he was one of the pioneers of X-ray in York and I remember he had one or two fingers missing because of the X-ray business.

I had a very happy childhood because we were on the fringe of the country. Where Burton Stone Lane council estate is now, they were all fields. We had lovely flowers in the meadows, buttercups and all sorts. And lots and lots of birds – yellow hammers and green finches – and butterflies and it was one of our joys to go along the hedgerows. We had a matchbox and we would pick the caterpillars and put them in.

We didn't travel about a great deal but I did have nice holidays. One of my great-grandmothers had a confinement at Beningbrough Grange. And we became great friends of the family and my brother and I used to go for holidays. I remember Mr Rockcliffe, he'd come into York to the market and pick us up on the way back in the horse and trap, and we'd go clippity-cloppit up the A19. It is full of cars now, but on an autumn evening it was really beautiful and you could hear the horses clippity-clop and the owls hoot.

Mary Barnes, born 1912

Only One Mother

Mother did the baking, we never had much bought stuff in our house. She was a trained dressmaker and I've never worn many shop-made clothes, I learned to make me own. There was a little verse:

> 'You've only one mother
> Compare her with no other
> She is gentle and forgiving
> Prize her while she's living
> You have no friend like a good mother
> From the cradle to the grave.'

That just fits my mother. She was the best anybody could have. My father was very strict but he was kind. It was the nearest way of living like God that you could get to be. If he said you could have a thing, he would move heaven and earth and he would still get it for you. But if he said 'no', there was no way round him, he'd just say 'no' and that was it.

Eliza Kirby, born 1891

In The Orphanage

Through a child's eye, growing up in an orphanage, you view things differently. You knew from the word go, even if you didn't think about it every day, it was at the back of your mind that your parents didn't want you. And you had to develop a personality, to come to terms with life. When you left the homes, they'd give you a portmanteau with all the clothes to start on, and that was the end of the road and you had to make your own way after that. As a baby I was supposed to be left at the Elms, wrapped up in brown paper and on the doorstep. I went to St Hilda's in Lowther Street and I was there up to being about seven. Then I went to the boy's home at 120 Haxby Road, and from there to a home in Wigginton Road, and then to Feversham Crescent.

I was at Fairfield Sanatorium, with suspected TB. The boys would go to Filey and Primrose Valley, and Dr Crane would take me for the day and bring me back to the hospital.

Each boy had a job. I'm speaking in terms of about twelve boys in each home. You did the washing up between you before you went out. Friday was work night and I remember these hessian aprons we wore, they used to let us polish the floors. In all the homes I was in, there was the same sort of routine. You had the day room where you played. And at Feversham Crescent,

Children from St Hilda's Home, late 1940s. Superintendent Mary McGuire is on the second row, sixth from left.

A trip to the coast for the children of St Hilda's Home, c. 1950.

it was certainly very vivid, with a good sort of parquet floor.

There'd be two dormitories with six boys in each. And I always remember Miss Gunner 'cos she rather favoured me, she took that extra bit of care because I was nervous of thunder. And they had an older boy to look after a younger boy, he was in charge to make sure that you cleaned your teeth and were properly washed. But there was an element of cruelty running through. A bit physical but more mental. If a boy had been naughty, this was when Mrs James was the head, you'd get four strokes of the cane across your fingers. And if you wet the bed or anything, they'd rub your nose in it or they'd lock you in the coal house for two or three hours.

We had a cat in the home called Binkie, and I had a love for Binkie, the little tortoise shell cat but living in the homes has left its mark on me, you got the accommodation but beyond that, you never got the love that a child needs, you see.

Wilf Cussons, born 1927

A Penny In The Bucket

Pocket money used to be a ha'penny a week and it was spent very carefully – usually on sweets or tiger nuts. There were bootlaces which were long thin strips of liquorice, and everlasting strips which were toffee that had been rolled out very thinly to a foot in length. And if we had more than a ha'penny, we would perhaps be allowed to go to the

The boys from St Hilda's.

Victoria Hall in Goodramgate. You went in the back way and dropped a penny in the bucket and sat waiting. Great cheers when the pianist arrived and then you saw the silent film.

Mrs S. H., born 1904

The Fever Hospital

In 1910 I had scarlet fever and went into Yearsley Bridge hospital and I was in over the Christmas period. We always had very happy Christmases at home, we never had many presents but it was happy. We had a stocking with an apple, an orange, nuts and a new penny, and if there was a gift it would be something to wear. I was in hospital over Christmas and I remember my parents were not allowed into the hospital because of the other children back home. We talked to them through a window. And I got a porcelain boot full of chocolates. I can see it now. That was absolute heaven to have something all of my own, something I'd never had before. And after eight weeks I came home and then one by one all the rest of the family went in with scarlet fever.

Mrs S. H., born 1904

The Hilly Fields

We would go out quite a lot in winter, sliding and skating, to the hilly fields opposite Terry's. There was a

16

big pond up there and it wasn't deep, it used to freeze over quite quickly. A lot of times we went to Rowntrees Park when that froze over, you were only allowed to go when the park keeper said so.

Ernest Armstrong, born 1914

Clifton Feast

Cussans's had a little farm at the bottom of Burton Stone Lane, and they had one daughter. Poor Angie, she didn't half have to work hard, lugging that great can of milk, and she had a pint measure and you'd go to the door with the basin. We lived at the bottom of Compton Street and I hadn't to go up to the top. And when I heard the sound of a motor car one time, I went helter skelter. I got into trouble for going so far up the street but I wanted to see it. Then there were the two-day feasts every year, first and second of May there was always the Clifton Feast on the

Green and there was hurdy-gurdies and roundy roundy things and swing boats. The roundabouts went too fast for me and I got dizzy. You could get on a horse, you sat on that, and they had to work it by hand and you got so many rounds for tuppence. You saved up for the Clifton Feast.

I've been across the river in the ferry for tuppence. The man generally seemed to be on the far side and he didn't seem to moor very often at our side. But if you went and clapped your hands, he'd soon appear from somewhere.

The horse trough on the green, Miss Husband used to look after that. She lived three or four houses from the top of Burton Stone Lane, she thought the world of animals and did a great deal of work for the RSPCA. And I suppose she engaged a man to clean the trough out once or twice a week. He used to go with a bucket and a broom and empty it, sweep it out and then it was refilled. The horses coming in from the Shipton Road, they didn't have to be told, they knew where it was. They used to pull up

The Fever Hospital, Yearsley Bridge.

Bootham, *c.* 1910.

for themselves, you couldn't drive them past, they'd always have a drink.

Old Donkey Norton had a little cart and a donkey and he had a marvellous voice. Dr Ferguson lived at the top of Burton Stone Lane and he was tickled to death when Donkey Norton used to shout, 'Potatooooooooes!' 'Do you want any 'tatoes this morning?' Or 'Tuppence a bunch of bananas'. They'd sell you oranges and apples and plums and everything that came in season. There was the coal man come round, with a barrow, and he used to shout, 'Coooool'. And the knife grinder used to shout, 'Any knives to grind?' and if you had any, you went to the door and they'd sort out everything for you.

I can remember when they first had lights in Bootham, I don't remember the year but they was so lit up. At first a man on a bike would go with a tall hook, and switch the light off. If he missed, he had

to wheel round and have another go. On a windy night they'd use a whole box of matches and then they didn't get them all lit. The gas-lighters assembled on those cobbles at St Crux church, I don't know if they signed on, I should think they did because they were all getting paid for it. And if I remember rightly a policeman used to come and give a little toot on the whistle, and then – whee! – they'd all scatter like anything.

I always wanted to go out with my father. He walked so fast that I was trotting. And if it was cold, I had a pair of wool gloves that my father gave me. But you still had cold hands and I used to go, 'Dad, my hand is cold'. 'Well come on, give it to me'. And he'd take my hand and put it in his pocket and that was champion. Oh I did love going out with my father.

Eliza Kirby, born 1891

Killing The Pig

It was usually Monday morning the pig was killed and the copper had to be hot, boiling and ready. They put it in salt and the sides and hams were all covered. We'd get a block of salt which was threepence and it had to be cut up and crushed. We did that in the washing tub and father salted the pig. Mother sorted out what she wanted for pork sausages and pies. And there was the spare rib and the chine. That has a thicker bone and a fat end. We used to enjoy that. The head of the pig was put in salt and then mother made brawn. She'd get two pounds of shin beef and put that with it and she made a nice potted meat and put it into basins. She made beautiful pork pies and never put the sausage into skins, we had sausage balls and they were lovely. And then when it was taken out of salt and washed thoroughly, it was hung up and we had hooks on each side of our windows in the kitchen. It took a few weeks to really dry out before we could cut into them. And mother would get the carver and cut a big piece off and put a tin in the oven and it would spread like butter, it was so beautiful and she would roast it very gently in the oven which made it very tasty on bread.

The oven was a sheet oven and we would get a piece of wood and push right down. It was a great big fireplace and we could probe a scuttle full of coal on there and then we had a coal rake and just when the fire wanted mending, we'd skip a bit of coal down with the rake. But that was when coal was fourteen shillings a ton, the best coal you could buy. It was called Park Hill coal and we got it from a man called Jim Lund and he had the best fuel. We hadn't any

other means of heating and mother had to make a jam on the fire and I know sometimes in summer when she'd be making jam, she had a big brass pan and it was as much as she could carry. It had to go outside to get cooled and she also made curds and sometimes she made what she called a hasty pudding in a smaller brass pan and we all enjoyed it.

When mother wanted to bake, she would get some bran out and make brown bread as well. Then she made beautiful bread cakes, both plain and currant and she'd say, often on Saturday after tea, 'Well I'm just packing a few tea cakes' and she made a few plain tea cakes, buttered for our breakfasts Sunday morning.

They had a real struggle had mother and father, but it was such a lot to be thankful for, that we always had plenty and were brought up to be honest and truthful. We had a big family but they had time to teach us what was right and what was wrong. We never went to bed without kneeling at our mother's knee and saying our prayers and then we always kissed mother and father goodnight. We had so much that money can't buy.

Eliza Taylor, born 1895

Going To Poppleton

At bank holidays, all Poppleton Road used to go to Poppleton. We had to walk and our mothers would pack a picnic. And then if you'd been good all day, very good, there was a little motor boat used to ply from Lendal Bridge to Poppleton called the *Mary Gordon*, it would perhaps be five pence. It was the highlight if your parents said you could come back on the *Mary Gordon*. If you went to town, the trams only came back to the Fox and you had to carry all the shopping up Poppleton Road. Then the Corporation started running a bus and all the housewives were out cheering it along, they were so delighted we'd got conveyance.

Winnie Mothersdale, born 1912

Our Own Entertainment

Father used to sing and when we were small he'd have me on one knee and Jessie on the other and would sing *Two Little Girls in Blue* and then he'd also march up and down singing *If you want to know the time ask a policeman*. And we'd play snap and dominoes and then the great day came when I was allowed

to stay up to play whist. The boys had been doing it for some time.

Ella Beswick, born 1906

Acomb before the 1930s

I was born in 1912 in Acomb and in those days it was quite a small village. It became part of York in the '30s.

Where there's Beech Grove and where the vicarage is leading into Carr Lane, that was fields, buttercups and daisies and lots of wild roses, and lots of larch trees which were cut down. When I was about ten there was an Acomb show every year. It was on for three days and they had tents with flowers and vegetables and prizes. It lasted until they started using the field for building operations. People came from all over and it was the beginning of Acomb turning into a large sized community.

Holgate Road and the Fox, *c.* 1933.

Front Street, Acomb in the 1930s.

There was no Clifton Bridge, we used Scarborough Bridge quite a lot, made a short cut to Acomb. I used to walk into Front Street sometimes to the shops, there was a baker's shop where one could buy nice cakes and sometimes when I got home from school and there didn't appear to be an awful lot for my tea, I would set off again and go into the village armed with sixpence and come back with a good bagful of cakes. I can remember on two occasions being threatened by a child to give up the money and so of course I came back crying because I'd lost my sixpence and I'd no cakes, and that made me a bit wary. There was always a rough element in the village, I think if they saw you wearing a school hat and school uniform, they tended to have a go at you.

We used to go to Scarborough twice – two weeks in the year. It was quite an event. We stayed in lodgings where we bought food and the landlady cooked it. I can always remember on the day of arrival it was very exciting. There was a big difference in the class structure then. We were in lodgings on the North Shore, they were very pleasant, but the South Cliff, which is where the Grand Hotel is, was always full of wealthy people. And the Spa was the place to go. They had a Sunday morning parade where people paraded around with parasols if it was hot, Edwardian style, and really dressed up. If you go to Scarborough now you don't see that division. We went by train and we got to the station and there were horse-drawn things. There was no other mode of transport so every train would be full.

Irene Seymour James, born 1912

21

Daddy's Girl

I was born in 1919 when my father, William Percy Brown, came back from the war. He got a medal for gallantry. We were daddy's girls, he died when I was ten and we missed him a lot.

We lived at 17 Davygate until I was four years old and we moved to Scarcroft Hill. We had a semi-detached house with eight bedrooms. There were my mother and father, my sister and I and the maid. We all had a bedroom, then the playroom, the box room and mother's sewing room. Mother would give bridge parties and whist drives. My father's friends came to the house and we'd start the evening by singing round the piano. He played a lot and would sing and some nights they played cards and drank port wine and smoked. I was allowed from an early age to stay up.

I went to St Margaret's school in Micklegate, a private school run by sisters of the Anglican church. I used to walk with my father when he was going to work. We wore maroon blazers and navy gymslips, cream blouses and a sort of cap. Then at twelve I went to boarding school in Harrogate. We took a furnished house in Robin Hood's Bay or Filey for the month of August, and took the maid with us as well. We'd go by taxicab to the station and we sent the trunk in advance so it was waiting for us when we got there. We did that until I was fifteen then we went cruising, round the Canary Islands or the Mediterranean.

We went to my grandfather's at Christmas out at Allerthorpe. We all went, my aunts and uncles and their children. We sat at a big table with a turkey at one end and a goose at the other. We always had a big Christmas tree. We used to get up early and go to church, the whole lot of us, and then in the dining room our parents had laid out all the presents in heaps for each person. I remember getting dolls and dolls' prams, a toy aeroplane that flew and useful presents like fur gloves. Then we went out with grandfather in his car. It was an open car and two of us could sit in the front with him.

Margaret Goldie, born 1919

Cleaning Father's Horn

My father was in the British Legion brass band, their headquarters were in Micklegate, and he played the French horn. In those days the instruments were made of ordinary brass and had to be polished. It's a conglomeration of twists and turns, and it was quite a job cleaning it with Brasso cloths. If he went in for any competitions or like Military Sunday when they paraded, they wanted all their instruments lovely and shiny. One of the boys had to clean the French horn for him before he went on parade and they got sixpence which was quite a fortune in those days!

Nearly every year the family used to go with the British Legion band to Blackpool for the championships, and I think that was considered the holiday of the year.

Ernest Armstrong, born 1914

CHAPTER 2

Happiest days of our lives?

Priory Street School, 1918.

Dancing at Priory Street School, *c.* 1920.

My Earliest Memory

My earliest memory was starting school when I was little more than three years old. I remember it was a very snowy day, and my father in his dinner hour coming to meet us and picking me up and putting me on his shoulder and then chasing home with me to get back to work within the hour. I had me dinner and then I just laid down on the hearth rug and fell fast asleep, and I didn't go back in the afternoon.

Elsie Fowler, born 1896

The Esperanto School

I went to a little school which was run by an ex-schoolmistress and she called it the Esperanto school and it had quite a few pupils. I was about four and a half and I stayed until I was eight. I was very happy there though I don't think I learnt much. You dressed up in fancy frocks and gave little concerts for the parents. Even to this day there are people who would like the Esperanto language to be universal and she was one of them at the time and she had lessons learning it which were no use whatever when we left the school, but she was a bit obsessed with it.

Irene Seymour James, born 1912

Priory Street School

We went to Priory Street school. I remember being whacked on the hand, the teacher lost her temper and got cross with me and instead of using the cane she used a little pointer. She did hit it hard, I yelled terribly and the headmistress came downstairs to see what was wrong. I hated school. I liked the first half hour, the Scripture lesson, I thought that was beautiful. And I liked needlework, Monday and Tuesday afternoons. I won first prize three years in succession and it was a special prize the last year for neat sewing. We came in from Tollerton and one of the oldest boys and oldest girls was allowed to go at playtime and put the gas oven on low, and if you had anything in a tin, if your mother sent you with a meat pie, they'd put it in the oven for you and it was nice and warm by twelve o'clock.

Eliza Kirby, born 1891

Singing

At the end of term, we had the usual concert, when we were all expected to do a little something. I remember with my friend Elsie, we decided that we would sing. And we sang *Underneath the Gaslight Glitters* and put all our heart and soul in, but we were so pathetic that at the end of the performance we were told never to sing again, and that I should stick to recitation which evidently was one of my good points.

Ella Beswick, born 1906

One of York's most well-loved schools was St Clement's, always known as Cherry Street.

A Teacupful Of Water

At Cherry Street school I remember a lady coming to give us a lecture on how to keep ourselves clean and this left an impression on me. She had been a nurse in the First World War and related a story about how you could keep clean with a teacupful of water because they were always short of water. I had this vivid picture of her sitting over a teacupful of water getting washed, and she was of quite ample proportions I can tell you!

Mrs D. Cooper, born 1921

Cherry Street School

At Cherry Street school we started at three years old and I remember the headmistress, Miss Buckingham, a little grey-haired old lady, nice but strict. They took us for drill in the schoolyard and Miss Jarvis was very keen, she'd come round, 'Tuck your tummy in and put your shoulders back'. Then we had a headmistress from Loughborough and all we ever got was, 'You're not a bit like my girls at Loughborough'. She was always ramming Loughborough girls down our throats. We had to have clean handkerchieves and shoes, and with it being a church school, once a week the St Clement's rector came in to give us a Scripture lesson. The first one was Canon Argles. At Christmas when we had our exams, he would always give prizes to people for writing and arithmetic. I got one for writing, it was called 'Snow White'.

We used to go to church every Ascension Day. I couldn't go one time, I played hockey and I got me eye split. One of my friends thought she was playing golf and used a hockey stick,

Domestic work at White Cross Lodge, Haxby Road, 1930s.

St Clement's School (Cherry Street), 1920s. From left to right, back row: Miss Richardson, Violet Green, Gladys Collins, Mary Webster, ? Pollard, Hilda Eshelby, Edith Ward, Lily Ward, -?-, -?-. Middle row: Connie Charlton, Annie Cundall, Jessie Falkener, Dorothy Readman, -?-, -?-, Winifred Lickley, Audrey Nicholson, Gladys Wrigglesworth, Elsie Hawkes. Front row: Lara Pannet, Mary Bedford, -?-, Annie Foster, Irene Plummer, Muriel Lightfoot, ? Watson.

'Watch me send this ball across to our pitch on Knavesmire' and she swung and swung it and I got it right there, I should have had it stitched. But I liked hockey, once a week we used to play other schools. I got me legs banged a bit 'cos I wouldn't wear shin pads and I was usually centre half.

We wore a navy blue gymslip and thick black stockings, and pork pie hats with a badge on. We had long forms in those days, and desks joined together with little inkwells in each one. I was once the monitor and I had to go round all the classrooms, checking the attendance. On the board in front of every classroom I had to chalk on how many was in each class. Then Miss Judges came and she introduced drama and we used to act plays. She was getting an old lady and she'd sit with her leg up with a big bandage on her foot. Once I knocked an easel onto her foot, she had it on top of the chair and she nearly went mad. Once we had a play and I had to be clumsy and carry a baby around. I had to carry this doll up the steps and she shouted at me 'cos I wasn't clumsy enough. I slipped and fell and she thought I was pretty good, but I never intended falling.

For cookery lessons we'd go to White Cross Lodge, Haxby Road. The cookery mistress was called Miss McQuisten, she was Scottish. We made a Christmas cake once and used to make soup. It was nice soup, proper broth not like tinned stuff. Scots usually make nice soup don't they?

Lydia Emson, born 1909

Sweets for Sale

It was known as Micklegate Bar school, I was there 1923 to '29. Miss Patrick was headmistress and she was a lovely person. Her hobby was making sweets at home, and she used to bring them to school and sell them, and they were like cushions made of sugar, with some kind of fruit filling.

George Beckwith, born 1919

The Cricket Bat

Every so often at school when sports equipment got damaged, they used to sell them to any students that wanted to buy them. One of the cricket bats had a piece broken off the bottom, and I was able to buy it for sixpence. One of our Sunday school teachers was a joiner and had a workshop at the top of our street, over the entrance to a yard. I took the bat to him and he repaired it for me, by gluing and pegging it. It took a while to set but he did it for me and it didn't cost me anything, so I got a good cricket bat for sixpence.

Ernest Armstrong, born 1914

On The Way To School

I was going to Fishergate school one day and it was pouring with rain. There was a man on a ladder washing some windows of a public house and it struck lightning and this man dropped off the ladder. I heard the crash. He was dead. It upset me that much but I thought 'If I'm late, I'll get the stick'.

You always got the stick if you were even a minute late. But I thought I'd better go and tell them in this pub. The woman said, 'Sit down a minute' and I'm sure she gave me a drop of whisky! When I got to school the teacher said, 'Have you seen the time?' and wouldn't let me explain. She brought the cane out and gave me a stroke and I pulled my hand back so it didn't come down too hard so she gave me another then another.

I sat in the class and all of a sudden I started to cry from shock. She told me to sit outside. Our headmaster Mr Barker came out and he said, 'What's the matter with you?' so I told him and he said he'd never heard anything so horrible in his life. He went in there and shouted at that teacher and he said, 'She didn't need to come to school but she came and look at the reception she

got'. And he got someone to take me home.

But I loved learning. I passed everything when I was twelve, every class, and then you paid to go on. I loved school, I wasn't struck on holidays.

Nell McTurk, born 1896

Education Boots

At Micklegate Bar school we were taught how to write which was called penmanship. There was no such thing as ballpoint pens, and no calculators and all these modern things. We had fountain pens and you just squeezed a rubber thing and filled it out of the ink well. At four o'clock we used to sing *Now the Day is Over*. And there

Micklegate Bar, 1961. The school was the building immediately in front of the bar on the right, with trees behind.

Scarcroft School, eleven and twelve year olds, in 1908. Elsie Fowler is next to Miss Evans, a teacher.

was a charitable organisation that gave out boots and clothing for poor children. They got a nickname – education boots. They had odd nails in and toe caps and studs and when you got them on coming out of Lady Peckitt's Yard, clomp, clomp, clomp, I think they could have heard it the other side of York.

George Beckwith, born 1919

The Best Football School

I went to Poppleton Road school, best football school in England I should think. They used to win league and cup every year, for thirteen years they won both. Mr Appleby taught football. We had a good lot of internationals from

schooldays. One vivid memory was when they gave me a red tam o'shanter and I kicked it all the way to school. I didn't want to wear a lass's hat. I had a scholarship to Archbishop Holgate's where we used to have straw hats, starched with bands round and the Bishop's mitre on the front. It was pretty strict and I got the stick on the backside.

Walter Scaife, born 1903

Scarcroft School

It was a very good school was Scarcroft. It was well organised and well disciplined and you did as you were told. We didn't dare play teachers up. We were scared stiff of the headmistress,

29

she used to glare. I had a favourite for certain subjects, Miss Evans was the one that took us for English grammar, she made it more interesting somehow and I used to love the session of history with Mr Creegan. I could have listened all day. I liked poetry and I got 'excellent' for recitation. We used to have to stand up and we had Wordsworth's poems, 'The Daffodils', we had to go to the front of the class and recite them. Then the war broke out in 1914 and they took nearly all of the schools for offices. They were all turned out of Scarcroft school and the rest of their education was in South Bank Adult School.

Elsie Fowler, born 1896

Mill Mount Grammar School

Mill Mount was a fee-paying school but the bulk of the children were there on grants or scholarships. It was quite spacious, we only had the house as the school and we used the main staircase. I don't think latterly the pupils were allowed to use the main staircase, they had to use the servants' staircase, and the gymnasium was the old dining room and it still had the lift and all the accoutrements – it came up from the kitchens. We could decide for ourselves whether we used the bus or the tram. We bought tickets in bundles on Monday but it didn't cover every journey so sometimes we had to walk or cycle. But I did like the sports. We had a netball pitch in the grounds but it was cinder. The French mistress had learnt all her French in the arts side of Paris, Montmartre, and although her home town had been Leeds, she would have

looked far more at home in Montmartre. The others were mostly graduates and they were more dedicated, and of course none of them were married. If they'd got married, they would have left.

Irene Seymour James, born 1912

The Girl At The Window

In Ebor Buildings in Bedern they were nearly all Catholics and they went to St Wilfred's school. There used to be a girl who'd stand at her window and she had long dark hair and she'd stand plaiting it and I'd think it was because she was a Catholic that she was off school a lot. I used to think, 'I wish I was Catholic so you don't have to go to school as much' but I realised as I got older that she was probably minding the children while her mother worked.

Doris Lonsdale, born 1907

It Sank In The Middle

I liked St Clement's even though it was perhaps old and musty. Miss Richardson was one of my favourite teachers. The headmistress owned a tiny car. She was a large woman and we all used to laugh outside school when she climbed into the car and it sank in the middle.

I remember one teacher rapping me on the knuckles for not being able to do joined-up writing. It couldn't have been a very good way of teaching, as to this day I still have not mastered the art!

Irene Plummer, born c. 1919

Elsie Fowler, aged seventeen in 1913.

St Clement's School (Cherry Street) Standard 4, *c.* 1915. On the second row back are: Ethel Wildon (far right) and Madge Wildon (second from right).

Back From Argentina

My eldest brother, George Wildon, went to live in Argentina to work on the railways about 1910. His two daughters, Madge and Ethel, came home on holiday in 1914 and when the war broke out, they had to stay in York for the next few years. They lived with us and were more like sisters because Madge was only eight years younger than me. They went to Cherry Street school. Later they went back to South America and Madge married Senor De La Rosa and Ethel married Norman Coggan, the cousin of Donald Coggan, who was Archbishop of York at one time.

Nell McTurk (née Wildon), born 1896

CHAPTER 3

Goin' courtin'

Ashton family. Elsie Fowler's grandfather, David Ashton, is seated. Standing on the left is his son William, standing on right is his grandson David, and at the front is his great-grandson David.

Strict With The Girls

In our house the men were very strict. My grandfather, a farmer, said, 'I'll shoot the first fellas that come after my girls'. And it's all so different today; for us old ones it's a lot of taking in.

Elsie Fowler, born 1896

Raking On Sunday Night

Raking up and down, we used to call it, from Scarborough Bridge along the riverside into Coney Street, there was quite a lot. Used to wave and shout at each other. Everybody went raking, there was nothing else to do. The girls used to go showing off to the boys, walk about giggling and carrying on, 'Ooh look at him'. Many a romance started from raking. But you never went under Scarborough Bridge, you kept out of the way, only daring ones went under the bridge. It was pitch black, you don't know who'd be there, girls used to scream if a chap got hold of them.

Vera Thomlinson, born 1916

Meeting The Boys

The first boy I went out with used to see me home and that sort of thing, that didn't last long and then we'd go out in groups, maybe half a dozen of us

Lendal Bridge and river bank, 1927.

and we paired off. We used to dance a lot in those days at the Folk Hall, the De Grey Rooms or Assembly Rooms. You'd go to dances and take care of your appearance, get a pretty dress, that sort of thing. Not a lot of make-up, a bit of lipstick and powder and that was it. People used to meet on the Monkey Parades. In summertime you'd go to the Mount on Tadcaster Road and on the Esplanade, by the river and that's how you got to know each other, a lot of people started courting through these meetings and eventually got married.

I started going out with my husband when I was about twenty-two, and we had a happy courtship. North Eastern Railway ran trips and you'd go to Coxwold, get off the train there and walk up onto the moors for the whole day and then meet the train again and come home. We played tennis a good deal 'cos there was a lot more courts than there are now. We could go into Wigginton Road, Glen Gardens up Heworth, Rowntrees Park and Scarcroft, in summertime, two or three nights a week. And there was swimming in the river. We used to have lovely picnics, about twenty of us, there was such a lot of fun and bounce. Linton Locks had nice sandy banks and you could dive in there, it wasn't muddy. I eventually paired off with my husband, the war was looming up and it was like a shadow. But we'd go for walks and do a bit of canoodling, there's some nice walks round York and it was a nice gentle courtship. Much more romantic. You were a long time before you held hands and ages before you had a kiss and now they meet and it's into bed after about an hour or two, which to me isn't a bit romantic. Maybe we were a bit sheltered

but I don't regret having a romantic courtship, it was a lot nicer. When you'd been going out with a boy a few times, you'd take him home for Sunday tea, to be vetted so to speak. It never happened to me because my parents knew my husband and his family, it was a boy-next-door sort of thing and it worked out all right. We had little tiffs, I don't believe any married couple who say they never had a tiff, they're living in cloud cuckoo land if they say that. We had occasional rows but we were happy and we never looked at anybody else, either of us. He proposed to me at one of the dances at the Folk Hall. When we realised war was coming, we thought we would like to get married before he went into the Army. We got married on 9 March 1940 and he went in the Army on 15 March and came out again in November 1945.

Mary Barnes, born 1912

Nothing Cheeky

We had a bit of a laugh but they never did anything cheeky. At that time they weren't a bit like they are now. If I'd gone home and said, 'I'm going to live with this bloke for two years before we get married', my mother would have gone in a mental home, I think. I can honestly say that when we went camping, none of the lads ever wanted to come in the tent where the girls were. There was no cheek, it's just altered since the war. We daren't go home and say you'd got into trouble, I think I'd have drowned meself if I had.

Mrs C., born 1909

Eva Guyll with husband John, and children; Peter aged seven, Val aged four, and twins John and Jean aged two, 1944.

I Tripped Her Up

I met my wife when I was fifteen. She was chasing her sister round a tree and I put me foot out and tripped her up, and down she went. I says, 'Look, do you want me to take you out tonight?' She says, 'You're the last one I'd ever think of coming out with'. We've been married forty-seven years.

George Beckwith, born 1919

Shilling Dances

We used to go to shilling dances at Tang Hall pavilion. I was pretty handy at doing hair and on Friday night I'd have three or four girls down to tong-wave their hair for the dance. I met my husband at a dance at New Earswick. We'd act a bit giddy and he'd

trip himself up and I'd say to my friend, 'Silly looking beggar. He's daft'. I never realised I'd end up with him. I was courting five years before we got married. Him and I used to go sometimes to Scarborough, there was night trips on a train then. But we didn't go away an awful lot really. We had our bikes and we used to cycle a lot or go up river on boats on a Sunday and have a picnic at Bishopthorpe.

Eva Guyll, born 1914

Singers In The Choir

I met my husband at a carol singing party. There were lots of social activities in connection with the church, and we were both in the choir. We belonged a tennis club too, so wherever we went we were thrown into each other's company, although we were six years before we married. Happy days, he was a wonderful man.

Mrs S. H., born 1904

Kissed At The Gala

It was a wonderful thing was the York Gala. Every house was decorated and there was a marquee for the flowers. When you went in you could smell them. I'd never had boyfriends, only when I met John. I met him at the Gala – I was eighteen, the first time kissed.

Polly Preston, born 1902

Down Lovers' Lane

I was in service at St Peter's school at fourteen and I went to post some letters and I dropped them and he come from the other side of the road and picked them up for me and that's how I got off with him. We had one night off a week and I used to go home to stay. We'd go to St George's Field to watch the band and then my father used to be coming along to find me. We were supposed to be in by ten or we got no supper. When we were courting we'd go to King Street fish shop and get one of each and peas in a bread bun for tuppence, or we'd go up Wigginton Road where all the fields were and then down Clifton to Lovers'

York Gala, 1909.

Chez Pierre, Stonegate hairdresser in 1934.

Lane. Once we were stood by a back door saying goodnight and it flew open and I fell in and landed on me back. The lady came out to us but she just said had I hurt myself? The dustman had been and he hadn't put the bolt on.

Edith Harton, born 1901

Make-up In The 1930s

We didn't go and get our hair done like they do now. I can remember sending away for a make-up pack, but you could always tell when people used it – they never thought about colours, just had bright red lips and powder on. We never went dancing much but girls that went dancing had their hair flat like an Eton crop. I never had mine cut like that, I can remember having it cut and singed, but there were girls that were a bit more adventurous. We had lisle stockings, I'd think, 'If only I could have a pair of silk stockings'. I had a younger sister and she went to work doing aeroplane blades at Hills, and I can remember her having nylon stockings when they first came out. I was busy saving to get married so I missed out on those sort of things – I can remember her having lovely silk cami-knickers.

Vera Thomlinson, born 1916

All For Two Fresh Eggs

Arthur Whittington, they called him, he was a real nice lad, same age as me, fourteen. He worked in Terry's bakehouse and that's how I met him. I said to me mother, 'Can I go – a young man wants to…' and she says, 'No you can't'. I says, 'Well he's bringing you two fresh eggs'. 'Oh you can go this time'. Well we were coming down the road and I had an umbrella, and I ran up the railing and I broke the umbrella in two. Me mother was waiting at the top of the street, 'Where have you been? You've had time to get home before this!' I never went again. Still she got the two eggs!

Gertie Hutchinson, born 1906

On A Sunday Afternoon

We used to go up the Mount on a Sunday afternoon. Sometimes there was a band on the Knavesmire and you had a talk and you met girls. There was no rowdiness or aught, they used to like getting dressed up in those days. Decent suits, blue as a rule. My mother had three lads and we all had straw bangers, straw hats. I remember me mother taking us to a tailor in Goodramgate, they called it Fitwell, and she bought us three blackcloth blue coats. She knew a lot about cloth, she did dressmaking a bit at home.

Mr Kendrew, born 1902

He's A Soldier!

We were at the Victoria Hall and these two Scots Greys sat behind me and my friend and we walked home with them. And they asked us to meet them. I daren't go because soldiers were supposed to be the rogues of the country but he said, 'I'm a soldier because my mother died and me dad married again and I didn't like her so I joined up.' I sweethearted him and he went to war. I was in hospital with appendicitis when war broke out in 1914 so I didn't see him go. Me friends all walked along with them to the station. They used to look lovely, very smart. Somebody told me sister that they'd seen me out with a

Gloves
Hosiery
Lingerie

Millinery

Frocks
Coats
Neckwear

" The Ladies' Shop "

CROWS' 6, BLAKE STREET YORK

Crows', the ladies' shop, Blake Street in 1925.

soldier and so I took him home to introduce him and he joined the Temperance. They used to give them a tot of rum when they were at the front but he'd give his to his nearest neighbour, he was staunch teetotal. He was on the Somme but he never had a scratch. We got married when he was on leave in 1917 and after the war we went to live in Scotland but he died two years later.

Nell McTurk (née Wildon), born 1896

I Don't Want The Little One

I went with a few friends to the fairground on Leeman Road and while we were on the roundabout, Geoffrey and his friend were stood watching. He was small and his friend was tall and I said to my friend, 'I don't want the little one'. They came across and spoke to us, they both had motorbikes which was quite a

Nell Wildon and George Edmond at their wedding in 1917.

Mr Kendrew's wife, Dorothy, in her back yard, off Nunnery Lane, c. 1920.

thing in those days. But it wasn't long before I changed my mind, Geoffrey kept coming round looking for me. I used to work quite late, till six o'clock on an evening and we would probably go out on his motorbike. It was only taxed from May to October, he didn't tax it in the winter. Mostly we'd just walk round Poppleton and sit on the seat by the railway crossing, or walk down the lanes to the river, you'd always meet someone else to sit and chat to. He always brought me some flowers. Being on Leeman Road we had no garden.

Often on Saturday night we'd walk round the market in the summer. There was eight lines of stalls up and down. Then we'd go to Leeds market and they'd get a bag and fill it with vases and dishes, you'd get the lot for half a crown and I'd come back on the motorbike hugging these things.

We'd go round all the country places, Harrogate, Dalby Forest, Brimham Rocks, we really travelled a lot because that was our pleasure, he'd just spend his money on the motorbike. We went to Scarborough and that was when he asked me to marry him, in the Italian Gardens. I had a bottom drawer and we started to make rugs on winter nights. We got married in 1939 and we'd gone on holiday to Scarborough. While we there the war broke out and it didn't develop into a holiday, and I was glad of the motorbike to come back home on because the trains were just bringing evacuees.

Vera Thomlinson, born 1916

Dulcie and Ernest Armstrong's wedding at St Philip and St James, Clifton, 1941.

Wartime Wedding

I was called up on April 30th 1940 and we had to report to Leeds and they said we were going to Richmond and I didn't see Dulcie for six months. I used to spend most of my spare time either reading or writing letters to Dulcie. We got to know we were going abroad so we had a week's leave and we got married in July 1941. We were moved up to Scotland and Dulcie used to come up and stay and I got her a little room. I finally went abroad in December 1941. I finished up in India.

Ernest Armstrong, born 1914

Vera Thomlinson at the seaside, June 1933.

CHAPTER 4
The world of work

Anne Sturdy (centre), with friends at Scarborough in the 1920s.

Mrs Brown was one of the first women to work at the railway carriage works during the First World War.

The Carriage Works

I was on a drilling machine. We started at six o'clock in the morning and finished at five. My machine was a hand one, you put in what you were drilling, clamp it down, put the drill in. They were all stamped with a pin print and you had to get hold of a handle, pull the rail down while the strimmer went through the hole. That's all we did all day long. There was only five of us doing drilling, and four in the screw gang. Mr Bulmer was our charge hand and then there was Mr Goodhall. They were all elderly men but they were lovely.

I met my husband there, he was in the paints lab. We used to see them at dinner-times, and I went out with one or two before I went with him. He only got four shillings a week so we didn't go very far, just walked round Clifton Ings. He had to do seven years apprenticeship, while he was twenty-one. After he had finished, he did linings, rubbed them down and varnished them. They were lovely when they were finished. The trains used to have one long corridor along the carriage.

Margaret Brown, born 1900

The Between Maid

I went in service as a between maid. You work with the parlour maid first thing in the morning from half past six till breakfast, after breakfast you work with the housemaid till lunchtime, then in the kitchen with the cook. Never a slack moment. And they always had the carpets sent away for cleaning once a year so we had to keep them clean during the year. There was no carpet soap in those days. We used to have a rough cloth, a sponge cloth and then dust your carpets and dry them. There was a copper in one corner of the kitchen and you filled that with cold water then lit the fire and waited till it got hot. That's why you had to be up early on wash morning. I liked a peggy stick better than the posser, you should never splash it over the edge of the tub, we had a good big wooden tub, and a zinc tub, and an old fashioned wringer with wood rollers. We had a good backyard and we'd put the line out and when we hadn't the line we'd about three clothes horses.

We had to do blackleading every morning. But we didn't burn such big fires at home, it was much easier because you put your little lick of blacklead on, and then you had special brushes and you'd brush it off first with one brush and then finish it off with the clean brush and it would shine like the stars on a frosty night. A nice clean bright fireside makes all the difference.

Eliza Kirby, born 1891

The Cattle Market

We lived in the Spotted Cow but father's main interest was in the hay and fodder business. Nothing was thrown away in those days and we had

Pens adjoining the cattle market, with the Spotted Cow in background, *c.* 1909. The cattle drovers have long sticks.

proper milk cans and always kept a cow of our own, to get milk all year round. We had an ostler, Alf, who'd come on a Monday and bring the horses and traps in the stables. The Yorkshire cows were very distinctive, they had a reddish leg and some red on the face, but the backs and sides were white with a red mottling.

In 1923 or '24 there was a terrible outbreak of foot and mouth disease and the cattle market was closed for months. And we got it. They came to kill umpteen bullocks and the horses were hidden away and we were banished to the attic and we took the dog up, because they shoot them when they get foot and mouth, and they burn them. Dad used to say, 'You're not going in the buildings and among the cattle with Trixie', and we got this idea that she

would get shot and burnt like the cattle. It was like the miner's strike, it put dozens of people out of work. It was sad because no cattle was moved about, cows and pigs and sheep, anything with a cloven hoof. They still do this, stamp an order on all the farms, all movement of stock and they take them in these trucks.

I remember Tom Hall, he was a hedger and ditcher and he cut haystacks up. It wasn't baled then, it was made into haycocks, swept up and carted and put in stacks of varying sizes. He was quite a marvellous man and they had a hay spade which they carried on their bikes, it was shaped like a heart down to a point and a great bevelled edge, sharp as a razor, then a wooden ledge and a handle. They could cut wedges out, I presume it's like cutting peat. They used to buy hay in bales for the pens in the market, and they were tied up with string. I used to drive the horse on the hay rake and collect it up into swathes and they made it into cocks after so many days. If the hay had been laid damp then it heated up, it would fire from internal combustion. Great excitement if a stack looked like firing, because it was a source of income was your hay. There were itinerants, and they could tell whether it was heating up and then they would send for Tom to cut the bales, and put them up in the hayloft, a marvellous place with great wide floor-boards. It was sold to the men that brought the cattle on the Thursday market.

There used to be bull sales. They were bringing a bull one day and it decided to be awkward when it got round Walmgate Bar and it was on a length of rope and a bull-ring in its nose, a most handsome thing, enormous, and it got off and wallowed through all this wet concrete up to its middle. Talk about a going on! All round the auction rings were these pens, really thick metal stanchions with thinner ones in between and they'd put one bull or cow to each one. When they got them in there they were done up like you see them doing racehorses, washed and brushed and their hair combed.

Anne Sturdy, born 1908

Terry's Chocolate Factory

I worked at Terry's for thirty-two years in the almond paste department, we used to do some beautiful work. And

Walmgate Bar, with remains of cattle pens, in the 1970s.

Grisdale's shop, 22 Coney Street, pre-First World War.

I'm not kiddin' myself up but you had to have a little bit of the artistic about you to do this fancy work. It was a pleasure to look at it when it was finished. We worked from half past seven to five, and after the summer holidays it was seven on a morning until nine at night for three nights because the chocolates weren't put in cold store, they were all freshly made. And we were on piecework, you got what you made. I thought one Monday, 'I'll have a real good go and see what I can earn' and I earnt just over £3. And our foreman Mr Broughton came to congratulate me because it'd never been earnt before. I couldn't have kept it up. It was just that one week when I really set me stall out.

I started at eleven shillings a week, that was the starting rate, and my mother gave me a shilling back and eight pence for the pictures and tuppence each way on the bus and that was me finished.

Winnie Mothersdale, born 1912

Grisdale's

I was born 1885. My dad opened a shop and I was the cashier in the Public Benefit in Market Street, a big shoe shop. And then I went to work at Grisdale's in Coney Street. I was there four years, cooking for about twenty every day. I liked that job. And she wept when I left. She says, 'I'm sorry you're going. You've never spoilt a thing yet'. Grisdale's – a mantle shop, coats and dresses. Ladies' things. I used to get some lovely clothes there. Get them at cost. When you worked there, they didn't like you to look slovenly.

Edith Tavinder, born 1885

The Rialto Sweet Shop

I was in the Rialto sweet shop and I used to do four to eight. We'd sell sweets and cigarettes separate. You'd close at half past seven when they'd all gone in t' film, and then you'd have to cash up and we had a cigarette book

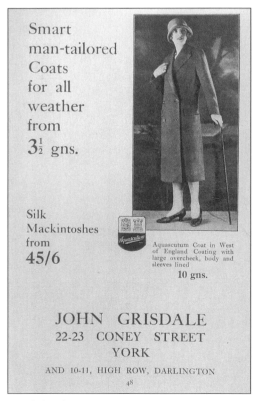

Smart man-tailored Coats for all weather from 3½ gns.

Silk Mackintoshes from 45/6

Aquascutum Coat in West of England Coating with large overcheck, body and sleeves lined

10 gns.

JOHN GRISDALE
22-23 CONEY STREET
YORK
AND 10-11, HIGH ROW, DARLINGTON
48

Grisdale's shop, 1925.

with our stock of cigarettes, and it had to tally with what the till roll was. It was hard work but I could do it in twenty minutes. I remember Frankie Vaughan coming and he was stood outside the shop and I just happened to go to the door and he was real small. I was amazed. And the Beatles come, and Shirley Bassey. I used to be able to go in and see 'em when I finished if I wanted. It was a skating rink as well at one bit, that was before I went to work there. I went skating once with some of my pals and I was always falling. I had roller skates and two chaps came and took over, and I went round and got off all right.

Eva Guyll, born 1914

The Nursemaid

There was an agency in Coney Street and her name was Mrs Stroud and I got this job through her. I went to Geoffrey Thompson, he was in the fertiliser industry in Skeldergate, and Mrs Thompson was related to the Churchills. We were living in this house called Bishopbarns in St George's Place. I was there six years. I brought up Dick and Christopher Thompson, and they were related to the Earl and Countess of Shipley. We always went to Salcombe for our holiday every year, in Devon. They had a house there and we'd go for the month but when we came back in 1926, the railway strike was on. It was midnight when we got back to York. We were travelling first class, but anybody came on when the strike was on and you'd to pull your own luggage out of the place.

Emily Fratsen looks after both baby and dog, 1920s.

When we went to Mayfair we were staying in Carlisle Square with a lady who was godmother to Dick. We went up in one of those old London taxis, but we came back in a red Rolls. And when we got into the hall there was a butler and Christopher took his hat off and held it out to him and he said, 'You have them well-trained'.

I wore a uniform, got it in Edgware Road, London. I was measured for it – a black hat, blue coat and a costume, silk blouse and long dark skirt. I could play the piano and I was caught doing it when the lady had gone out. And there was a new dance and Alice the parlourmaid came out and said, 'Shall we try that song again?' so we went down. The lady went out calling with her cards and she should have stayed out for tea but she didn't and we were in the drawing-room. She said 'What are

you doing?' and she just stood there and neither of us spoke. And she walked up to the piano which was a £300 Grand and took her knee and pushed the seat underneath. But she wasn't cross with us after that. They went out hunting and we used to go walking after them with the children who were dragging their ponies.

Emily Fratsen, born 1897

The Railway Strikes

Father was an engine driver, he was better off than most people. But I do remember when he was on short time, three days a week. He had to report seven days and he'd be sent home. Railway strikes were fairly frequent when I was a boy. I remember the 1919 strike. I'd be about seventeen, it was two years after the Russian Revolution and there was an awful lot of disillusioned soldiers about, and they'd no work. There were rebellious areas around us and the government of the day got a bit windy and when the strike took place, they had troops round the railway station and any point where there was access to the railway, and one place to get onto the railway was through the back yard of the Windmill Hotel on Blossom Street. I remember my father being stood there with a walking stick, it was a picket and the idea was to stop anybody who wanted to go to work down that passage. There was a policeman alongside him and a soldier with a gun.

There was the so-called Eyesight Strike. The engine men were told they were going to have their eyes tested under indoor conditions and they had to be able to read railway signals on posts and lights easily day and night. The normal test was out in the field testing them on the signals. That was the practical test, and they wanted to keep it.

Some of the railwaymen in those days couldn't read but they were marvellous engine drivers. It wasn't unusual for a man of seventy to be an engine driver. But the eyesight test was serious to the engine men. If they failed it, they came off the footplate. If their eyes were not

Emily Fratsen with Dick and Christopher Thompson on Blossom Street in the 1920s.

North Eastern Railway strike, August 1911.

right, they were put on cleaning duties. My father drove the engines between Newcastle and Grantham, and, in 1914, he had rather a special job, he had to take Lord Kitchener up to Newcastle. He didn't know where he was going beyond Newcastle but he actually went to John O'Groats. On that platform, Lord Kitchener walked up and gave my father and his fireman a tip.

George Thomas, born 1901

From Workhouse to Farm Boy

I was five when my father died and we all went in the workhouse and then they put us into five different homes. We never saw each other very much. I was at Haxby Road school and at playtime my sister came to the railings and says, 'Me mum's run away but we don't know where'. And I never saw her to this day. She went to London and we found out she died at Broadstairs.

When I was fourteen at Easter 1937, they gave me a case with clothes in and wellingtons and they said, 'You're going on a farm' and they took me down to

Piccadilly for a bus to Sunbridge near Bielby. I waited for ages and a chap came with a horse and cart with a lot of carrots on. I had to jump on the shafts and off we went. I got there and he told me to tip up the carrots and wash them and put the horse in and feed it. They told me to leave the case at the door and I thought I must be going into lodgings. We walked across this bit of field and he says, 'This is it'. A hen hut with two nails in for your hat and coat and a camp bed inside and that was it. I was pulling carrots from morning till night, seven days a week for sixpence.

Then I went to Terrington as poultry boy, I used to collect all the eggs, washing them and grading them, churning the butter and washing the red

tiled floors once a week with boiling soap and water. And there were rats everywhere. I could just see their whiskers and then I'd throw the brush. Once, as a punishment, I had to go ratting. The farmer's son had a lantern in one hand and a big stick. He'd go into the meal bin and outside was a big water tank and there was holes for the water to come in and you could go behind there in the dark and you'd see their eyes, the rats behind there. They had different barrels for oats, maize, wheat and everything. You couldn't see the tops of the barrels for rats.

George Bye, born 1923

The Man from Radio Relay

One of the things I fancied was Radio Relay, so I started work there as an improver, just gone fourteen. A pound a week!

Radio Relay started in 1934. In those days there was no such things as transistor radios – even valve radios were very expensive, and scarce. You had a central radio receiving station, with a big amplifier over wires and they sent BBC programmes down those wires. In your house you had a little box with a five position switch on. You had 'off', one was the home service, two was your light programme, three was a programme selected from foreign stations, and four was a spare.

In Parliament Street was the showroom, control room and workshop. There were something like 10,000 people on the relay system and everything was done on landlines. We used to amplify it and you picked up

Peter Binns in a Radio Relay van, c. 1948.

Peter Binns (second from right), with Christopher Stone (fourth from right) at York station in the 1950s.

Brussels and Dutch programmes, American forces network, that sort of thing. And from that it expanded into sound systems.

But it's not just a question of connecting two wires and sending it out to somebody's house. You've got the overhead wires, you've got to keep everything in phase right the way through. We had sub-stations in South Bank, Tang Hall, Acomb, Clifton and Bootham. They would pick it up from there, and boost it for the rest of the area.

We used to do Terry's, they had their own amplifier, and right through the factory they had speakers in for 'music while you work', and any announcements anybody wanted, 'cos you could link into a microphone. We did the sound system for the Regatta every year. Speakers in the trees, and amplifiers here there and everywhere, from Scarborough Bridge down to Lendal Bridge. Then Radio Relay changed its name to York Relay, and we got contracts to do. We did recordings for the BBC to send to the British forces network in Germany. We had a little recording studio in Parliament Street, a lot of folks were in the forces and you could come in and make a little disc and send it off as a Christmas greeting.

We used to go out doing a programme called *Home Flash*, and the interviewer was Christopher Stone. He was the first official disc jockey ever on BBC radio. He'd give a bit of a spiel, put a record on, they were 78s in those days. He was on the light programme, and we'd go

53

out and record it and try to make it into a half hour programme. We travelled the country: we did *Home Flash York, Home Flash East Coast, Leicester, Gateshead* and *Cleveland*. We always interviewed the mayor of wherever, the football team, and places of interest. Very similar to *Down Your Way*.

There were two of us, a feller called Fred Street, my immediate boss, who was the chief engineer and myself. We'd stand with a microphone, dogsbody for whatever Christopher Stone's producer wanted us to do. I used to thoroughly enjoy it.

Everything was done on a wax disc. Tape recorders weren't invented, what you had was an aluminium disc coated on both sides with wax. You'd polish it, and put anti-static stuff on, and the cutting head was a sapphire. From your microphone and your amplifier you'd feed it on and it used to wriggle down and put the grooves in the record. You could make an impression of it and then finish up with a proper 78 record.

We used to do garden fetes, that sort of thing, PA systems basically – people like Harry Corbett and Sooty, before he became popular. He was at Huttons Ambo first time I met him, the original Harry Corbett, before Sweep was born!

Then I went in the forces, did my national service and they held my job

Peter Binns (right) meets Harry Corbett (second from right) in the 1960s. The producer is third from right.

View from the top floor of the Radio Relay shop in Parliament Street, overlooking St Sampson's Square with its many cars, 1952.

open, as they had to do in those days, so I walked back into it. Things had advanced and we got involved in the old Empire, doing the sound system in there, and in the Rialto cinema for Mr Prendergast. He'd started his weekend shows then. You got your normal cinema sound, projectors at the back, onto your screens. Then at the side of the stage you had amplifiers for controlling the microphones. If the show was on a Saturday, we used to go on the Friday and Saturday morning and meet all the guys that were coming:

Gerry and the Pacemakers, The Beatles, Heinz…all the pop stars (I've nearly been mobbed a dozen times down there), and set the mikes up as they wanted 'em, set the sound levels, get it marked down, and then actually go for the show, and control the mikes and their equipment. Then Granada took over York Relay, because of the coming of television. I presume they looked at it this way – 10,000 subscribers, 10,000 people who are wanting to get televisions, we'll step in, and bang that was it, Granada took over.

The chief engineer used to do a schedule and we'd get the Dutch equivalent of their *Radio Times*. You'd pick an hour of non-stop music and make it into a full day until Luxemburg started at six o'clock at night with its English programmes. We had receivers with big aerials on the roof at Parliament Street, and you used to tune it in when it came to the right time.

The Duchess of Kent got married in York, and we did the sound system for that in the Minster. The idea was, we had speakers to broadcast it through the streets, and the camera guys were up on the top and down at the bottom with cameras, and we had some amplifiers just through the Minster door, and what they were after was the sound of the Minster bells when they were chiming. And the idea was to put a microphone in the bell tower, and speakers on the corners of the square towers. I nearly fell off the top, and if it hadn't been for one of the camera stands and me catching my finger on there and ripping my finger open on it, I'd have been off the top of the Minster.

It was transistor radios that killed it. You could buy 'em for ten pound, where they used to charge one and six a week for your relay. But it's not all died out, we did the County Hospital, City Hospital, Fairfield Hospital, Fever Hospital, all the installations.

Peter Binns, born 1933

Jack Smith moved to Heslington in 1951 after working on a farm in Alne.

The Woodman

We used to get hired for the year at Martinmas in November, and you'd to stop a year or you didn't get full wages. You used to get five shillings and that was fastening for the year. [Like a contract.] You'd stand in York market at the hirings and wait for someone to give you a job. I remember after I got married I went to Allerton Park and I got measured for two suits. One was thirty-five bob and t'other was fifty bob, and they lasted about twelve years. There used to be a tailor in the village for cord trousers, breeches and corduroy leggings, fifteen bob a pair. It was nearly all cord, it lasted longer, it was rough wearing. You could get a packet of Woodbines for tuppence then and a pint of beer for threepence. I had half a crown a week pocket money and I always used to go and watch wrestling and boxing every Monday night and get fish and chips for threepence

I was on the forestry on Lord Deramore's estate doing draining, ditching, planting and all the general repairs on the estate. I was there twenty-eight years. There was 3,000 acres. He actually lived in Heslington Hall. Then the RAF took it and he moved into the Manor House. He had one daughter and she got married so this estate was sold to Lord Halifax and I stayed on.

I was a farm foreman, a woodman, there was eleven of us on the farm and it was all horses and we'd start feeding them at five o'clock in the morning then we'd be out in the fields at half past six ploughing till six at night. We had everything – sheep, pigs, cattle. I just had one cow for meself, and a pig

Jack Smith in a wood yard at Heslington in the 1950s.

Heslington, pre-First World War.

and twenty hens. And that was part of me wages. Because I was foreman, I lived in the farmhouse. The woodman before retired, he'd lived in the cottage and then I came into it after he died. We did all the tree felling and planting and had to sell stakes and rails and make gates and fencing, and do the general maintenance on the estate. I loved it.

I used to drive the Landrover for Lord Deramore when they were shooting every Wednesday and Saturday and I drove the guns around. They were numbered one to eight and each one drew his number out (they changed numbers every drive) for the different positions where they stood, so that one man didn't get all the best shooting. I used to do pigeon shoots, six weeks, February to March. We'd get maybe twenty or thirty pigeons a night.

A lot's changed in the village. There was no university, no building at the back, and no Badger Hill, that was all farmland. Where the university houses are, that was Bleachfield Farm. I remember driving cattle down Spring Lane to the cattle market in Kent Street. It was all agricultural land then.

When I retired, I did two years part-time gamekeeping for Lord Halifax. You catch all the vermin and pen the pheasants up and get the eggs and sit them in the incubators and rear 'em, leave 'em for about eight weeks and then let them out, feed 'em every day. Maybe three or four thousand. They don't breed in the wild. Each man got one pheasant at the end of the day and all the rest were sold to pay the expense for the bush beaters and food for the pheasants. We had some poachers and we waited six weeks for them down in the wood and there were three of us and we pounced on them and caught them. One got two years and t'other got eighteen months in jail, and the friend that was with me got his head cut, he had seven stitches. They'd hit him on the top with a rifle.

You had some satisfaction of planting trees and seeing 'em grow up. We used to plant anywhere from 600 to 1,000 a day. If it's good growing you can plant up to 800 easily, and if it's rough you can't do as much, and only about 18 inch high. Then we had 'em all to keep weeded, take a scythe and moor round 'em. We'd plant 340 per acre. If a wood's planted as it should be, it all lines up and you see 16 lines of trees anyway you look.

There was plenty of work in those days, I was never out of work. Never have been. There wasn't the machinery, we needed the people then. I've done quite a few different jobs, and I used to do quite a lot of sheep shearing, three and six to clip twenty sheep. That'd be in the 1930s. They have electric motors now. After the war they got more machinery and wanted less men and less cattle feeding, it's all artificial feed now. On modern farms it's all computerised.

Jack Smith, born 1910

Charles Minter was born in Kent and came to York in the 1930s. He recalls some outstanding events in his childhood, then his job in York.

City Engineer

I saw Bleriot fly the channel, saw him land in England, first man to fly the channel. My father said to me the night before that this man was flying to Dover, so I had to get up early to cycle over to see it, about twelve miles. I was selling papers, collecting the evening papers from the village station when the *Titanic* was sunk. Evening papers, ha'penny each. When I was a boy I worked at a baker's shop in the village, evenings and Saturdays, went around with bread in remote places. In the summer I used to have a basket made up with sweets in bags and ha'penny buns and I'd walk to the hop groves and sell them to the women who were picking

Charles and Edith Minter marry in 1922.

Charles Minter at a civic occasion, 1936.

hops. I earnt tuppence in the shilling commission and one week I earned a half sovereign.

I got a job in York as a planning assistant in the mayor's office. I was the only one, no staff at all. I was in the engineer's department and I went in for the planning examination and got that and then I was in the deputy engineer's room and he retired and I got his job. Then the superannuation act came out and my boss had to retire, he was over seventy and they recommended me to follow him. They advertised the job and there was a shortlist and I was appointed City Engineer in 1935.

We did everything then – planning, sewage disposal, architecture and were even responsible for the rooms in the Mansion House and the staff. Then the war came on and we had to go into rescue work. One of the jobs I had to do

Clifton Military Bridge, 1953.

60

Clifton Bridge being built, under the watchful eye of Field Officer Michael Wall, in the 1960s.

was take out the tram tracks. They gave me £25,000 to do it with and the war was so imminent, we sold the rails in the street as we dug them up, to merchants and we finished the job just inside the £25,000. There wasn't much construction work going on during the war. It took a year to remove the tramlines, they tried to fill them in with bitumen but a girl was killed, she came off her bicycle and got caught in the tramlines and got run over so that made them do something about it. They bought some trolleybuses for the Heworth run after a bit, those with the rubber tyres.

During the war there were house repairs but after the big raid they had contractors in from all over the place, no contract, just get on with it and put the roofs back. After the war we put a new pumping station down at Fulford for the sewage. We did all the work at Naburn, new filters and things, £300,000 worth and got it all up to date. We had floods, of course, which always caused a bit of bother, and snowfalls.

The Army built a bailey bridge over the river at Clifton and it was so popular that they left it up for two or three months but it had to go eventually and then there was such an outcry so we designed Clifton Bridge in the office and it was built.

Charles Minter, born 1897

W.P. Brown's

The business was started in 1891 in Nessgate by my grandfather Henry Rhodes Brown. It must have moved quite quickly into St Sampson's Square. In 1919 he decided to go into the wholesale business in Hope Street where they made underwear and aprons and overalls and he had a fleet of cars that used to go into the countryside to village shops carrying these goods. He had this until he died in 1936.

My grandfather was eccentric. He was brought up in the Blue Coat School. He never owned a coat or hat or gloves and he always rode in an open car all year round and he sat in the front with the chauffeur who was his nephew. He never liked to eat inside, he had all his meals in the garden, weather permitting, or just inside the French windows on a plain table where the maid served his food. When he was

Lord Mayor he showed me round the council chamber, that would be when I was twelve. We used to go and play in the Mansion House.

The shop was at the corner. At the beginning we had five young girls, only in their teens, fourteen when they started. The staff were very fond of my father. He used to play chess with one of them. By the time he died he had men working for him as well and he had taken in several of the other shops. In the late '30s there were about fifty there, including people doing alterations. The women of York seemed to like him and when he died they were lined up at the cemetery. When he got put up for the council it was a slum area in Hungate, the Guildhall ward, and they said he'd never get in because it was a Labour area. We went round canvassing. My grandfather used to stand in Exhibition Square on a box. That's how they used to handle

Davygate. W.P. Brown's is to the left of the horse and cart, c. 1910.

elections. I remember they were advocating a rise in the old age pension and he said a pound a week was adequate and someone stood up and said, 'It wouldn't keep your wife in hats'.

Near the store were two pubs knocked into one – the Angel and the Black Bull. The Black Bull was where they had music hall, there was a stage and performers had to go through the stage up a staircase to the dressing room at the back which was a small room with no windows. It was empty when we bought it. There were posters everywhere of past events. I don't know when it closed but the newspapers on the shelves had 1932 on them. When my father died, his brother took over, Henry Rhodes Brown, the same as his father. It was in the time of the Depression. He used to close the shop for a day and each hour in that day, he sold merchandise at bargain prices, and they could pay cash and it was popular with the women in York. They'd probably get half price corsets. I think they were mainly working-class people in those days and later on the farmers started coming in.

I worked there as a shop assistant for a short time in 1938 before I got married. I got twelve and sixpence a week, but they'd got seven and six in my father's time. We worked long hours although our parents said it was nothing, from eight thirty in the morning until six at night, Wednesday we finished at one and Thursday we finished at seven thirty and on Friday and Saturday we worked until eight unless there was a sale on, when it was nine. On a Saturday night at eight o'clock all the girls used to line up at the washbowl, just wash your face, straight into your party dress and out to the dances.

Margaret Goldie, born 1919

More New Babies

When I did my Health Visitor's training, you worked for the local authority and did one area. I did Bishopthorpe Road and Fulford Road right out to the city boundary, and we all had bikes in those days. It meant if you were going to visit new babies, which you did on the fourteenth day, I had to plan all my work for Bishopthorpe Road and then new babies on Fulford Road I'd see in the afternoon. Otherwise you were pedalling miles for nothing. I used to see Dr Crane, she was the first woman Medical Officer of Health in the country, and she said, 'You know Sturdy, you find more new babies on your district than anybody I know. How do you do it?'

You'd to explain about injections and they'd say, 'Oh I don't know, I don't make decisions like that, I'll have to ask me husband'. I'd call back when the husband was at home, they didn't often ask you in the house. Father would come out with his braces dangling down the back and he'd say, 'I don't believe in such new-fangled ideas. Now bugger off and don't come back'. Each visit took a long time, knocking on doors and explaining who you were. Dr Crane said, 'Have you done much good with the immunisation?' I'd say, 'I feel like the Kleeneze brush salesman'.

Anne Sturdy, born 1908

Vivian Stuart in the 1950s.

A Lady Novelist

My mother was born in 1918 and it was a privileged background. When she was about eleven she had encephalitis lethargica (sleeping sickness) and they never thought she would recover. She was told that either she'd have a brilliant brain or the opposite, and she had a brilliant brain. She went to Hungary to take a medical degree and, while there, helped Jewish friends and got money out for them. That part of her life was quite adventurous. She would bring her Rolls Royce car out and she would come wearing a corset with money packed in it.

We moved to Hopgrove in York and it was then that my mother started to write. She lived in York from 1952 to 1986. She considered York her home. She had a very courageous dog and sent a short story about the dog, and won a competition with Thompson Lane. It was literally bread and butter, she had to start somewhere. She got ten pounds.

Then they commissioned a romantic novel to be published in serial form. They expected her to write the first chapter and a synopsis in a fortnight, but by the time he came, she'd written the whole lot. She went on to write for DC Thompson, then she joined Mills & Boon in the early '60s. She wrote about three novels a year until she wanted to write about South Africa, a controversial anti-apartheid theme, and M & B wouldn't publish it so it was published by Robert Hale. She had by that time started the Romantic Novelists's Association with Ursula Bloom, Barbara Cartland and Denise Robins. She also wrote *The Beloved Little Admiral* about Harry Keppel which was a turning point in her career and then she wrote about Sebastopol and the Indian mutiny.

The Indian mutiny was factual. She had spent a lot of time in India and we had a bearer who we kept in touch with until he died. He had his letters written in the market and had to pay for them to be written. Mother shot crocodiles which now you wouldn't mention. She was a good shot, because everything she did she wanted to do well. She shot tigers but these were old tigers who went to the villages and killed the menfolk. She went on a banana boat and travelled to China and went to the earthquake city. My mother then went on to write about Australia, a totally different angle to her writing. It was a saga, to be twelve novels, starting in the 1700s.

She had a lot of energy and she was very strong. If you wanted anything from her, you had to take a cup of coffee up and placate her and if she had people who wanted to talk about medals or writing, you had to sit and be quiet. We did have a nanny who was able to cook so mother was able to work from nine o'clock until about eight. She did it as a job, she had no money then and she said literally, 'I have to write to earn a crust'.

She would write about seven hours a day if she stopped for a meal. She never

Smith's bookstall at York station, with a display of Vivian Stuart's books, 1960s.

Maurice Frankland, farmer of Lime Tree Farm, Heslington, 1937.

wrote by hand, she did it straight onto the typewriter with one finger, it was always an old Imperial. Sometimes she would take lunch off and exercise her dog and try to do things that would give her a break from the bedroom. She later moved and had an office, but she didn't consider material things important and she didn't acquire things, she was inclined to pass them on to somebody else. From a privileged background this was quite an unusual trait but her writing was the most important thing to her.

Mother wrote about seventy-six books. She started off as Vivian Stuart for Herbert Jenkins, and then she was Alex Stuart for Mills & Boon. But when she wrote *The Exiles* about Australia, she was William Stuart Long. Once she

got into it, they announced she was a woman. With the Australian series, they used to have a list of who sold the most and at the time of *Spycatcher*, she was above him. The York Writer's Circle have got a Vivian Stuart cup that they award to the winners of a competition.

Jenny Gooch, born 1936

Lime Tree Farm

My father was a tenant farmer on Lime Tree Farm in Heslington. It was dairy and arable, with cows and some pigs and crops. We had winter oats, potatoes, turnips and sugar beet. We had four horses. Joe and Wally were the two horsemen and my uncle used to

Joe Authbert with horses, at Lime Tree Farm, 1937.

Joe and Wally haymaking, Lime Tree Farm, 1937.

Village children potato picking, Lime Tree Farm, 1937.

love taking the Shire horses to the shows. They were groomed and exercised. Captain, Daisy and Royal. I can't remember the other one.

When my granny was living, there were eight in the family and two maids and five men living in the attics, and the bread and cakes and everything was made. I sometimes wonder how they coped with all that washing, there was seventeen living in that house. We had a separate wash house with a boiler and a great big washing line in the orchard.

The children from the village had a week off in October for potato picking and they could earn a bit of money. Men and women came from Tang Hall too, on the back of a wagon. They had white clay pipes and they'd pass one pipe round all of them. A machine loosened the potatoes and then they picked them off the surface.

The milking was done by hand, we had no electricity, just gas for light and cooking and a huge kitchen stove. Father was one of the first in the village to get a car, it was a Model T Ford and he sometimes took people to hospital or if anyone needed a lift anywhere. If there was a funeral, they came to father for his light wagon and horse and they'd often pay us in kind. We'd open the door in the morning and there were vegetables outside. We all helped each other and nothing was wasted.

There was something nice about that life, it was more leisurely, we could play in the village street at whips and tops because there was very little traffic.

Ann Harding, born 1922

CHAPTER 5
Sporting life

Clarion Cycling Club in the 1930s.

Alex McTurk as a boy, c. 1910.

Clarion Cycling Club

When I was about fifteen in 1929, four of us commenced the Clarion Cycling club. There was Alex McTurk, Bert Hepple and a gentleman called Helliwell. He was more retirement age but he was so interested in cycling that he joined up with us. And from that we gradually built up until we'd a membership of seventy. We met at Alex McTurk's house in Charlton Street, Bishopthorpe Road. The first outing was to Pontefract and Ferrybridge. After that we extended our distances until we got to Scarborough and Whitby. We formed three sections, one was the high rider section, 150 miles onwards, then the day riders which was up to 100 miles or more, then the afternoon riders who more often than not came to meet wherever the day riders returned to. It got stronger and stronger in York until it got so big that one or two members broke away and formed the Ebor Cycling Club. There was a good team, very little argument or ill feeling among them. I should say about a third were women. There was some quite good friendships made of it, as a matter of fact one or two of them married. I think some of the lads fancied their chances with some of the lasses and that was it. We went to Halifax to a meeting, and when we sat down to watch the meeting, first one started itching and then another, then one took his pants off and started shaking them in the wind and a matter of ten yards away, the women were doing likewise, unaware of us watching them. We'd sat down on anthills.

A few of us would go out for a ride on a Wednesday night too maybe fifty or sixty miles, maybe to Scarborough and back or up to Wensleydale. We had a president, a secretary and a vice-president. The rules were made up at Halifax actually. We rode in twos, captain at the front, sub-captain at the rear, and one in between that was keeping formation. If there was anything coming, a car from the rear, the sub-captain used to shout, 'Keep in'. With seventy cycles, you had thirty-five pairs which covered a fair distance, quite difficult for vehicles to overtake. We didn't adhere to main roads any more than we could help, because of the traffic. We used to have ports of call when we were returning from a run. One was Ma Green's at Scagglethorpe, coming back from the coast. Her husband was an AA scout and we were always made welcome there, tea and cakes and they were very reasonable. You could stop a couple of hours, she appreciated the company. And the other one was Gregson's of Thirsk, coming back from Redcar or Saltburn, and we'd have our tea there. He had a penny farthing and it was there for anybody that wanted a ride on it. The Clarion, their call was 'Boots', as a recognition for other club members and other sections. In summer we wore shorts and maybe an open-necked shirt and then in winter we had plus-fours and polo necked jumpers.
At that time there were two prominent dealers in York – Freddy Fenton and Arnold Elsegood. It was mainly Fenton's – he built the bikes, the Fenton 5, five pounds and the Fenton Zip, around eight pounds. They could be built to your own specification – Brunton hubs, Brough saddles, hinged forks, and then you had the racing tyres which were more of a sorbet rubber composition. You got a very good mileage from them. Without our support, his business wouldn't have thrived as it has done.

I went off to Whitby once and the Sleights bridge was broke down and the bridge was washed away wi' floods. We had to return to York and decided to go to Bridlington as an alternative, and by the time we got back, we'd had a longish day and were a bit saddle sore. You'd think nothing of going on a bike in those days.

Mr Raven, born 1914

Alex McTurk, still cycling in the 1950s.

Cycling party outside a teashop in Pocklington.

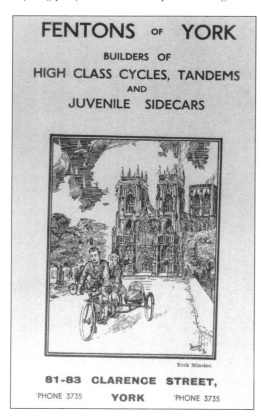

FENTONS OF YORK

BUILDERS OF
HIGH CLASS CYCLES, TANDEMS
AND
JUVENILE SIDECARS

York Minster.

81-83 CLARENCE STREET,
'PHONE 3735   **YORK**   'PHONE 3735

Fentons cycle shop in the 1930s.

The Highlight of My Life

The Clarion Cycling Club was the highlight of my life. I loved every Sunday. I thought it was seventh heaven, I'd never been anywhere before. When I did meet my husband, I says, 'I'm not seeing you on Sunday, I'm going out', so the poor devil had to go and buy a bike to come and catch me.

I was working all week and I wanted a bit of recro', and getting up on a morning's never been a trouble to me. If we were going to Halifax, I had to be in the market place by five o'clock. I was out everyday on the bike, but when I got this BSA, I thought I'd got the moon, thought I was a queen. I got a three speed fitted, the first one in York on a ladies' bike. But it wanted adjusting, we'd maybe be going round a corner and the chain came off and the whistle went, forty of 'em had to get off their bikes while I got mine fixed. I

Clarion Cycling Club with two tandems on Blubberhouses Moor.

had a lovely frame, one of those low bikes with a handle with four positions, 26 inch wheels and this nice derailer gear. It was just right, my size and I could put my foot down without any quick movements. I bought it from Russells, but Freddy Fenton fitted the derailer gear. They were about seven pounds and it took me five years to save it.

Down Blubberhouses was a nice ride on a bike in summer. And we used to have a paper chase in winter, on Boxing Day. They had different signs for us to follow and we'd go through farm yards, throw our bikes over the ditch and jump as fast, or get wet. I can still see us picking our bikes up and flinging them and getting over and next thing we're in the farm yard surrounded by geese and hens.

We did all the Lake District and stayed at hostels, a shilling a night.

We'd pack up on a Sunday and we could call at these cafés and they'd give you as much tea as you wanted to drink for fourpence. Once we'd been ever so far and there was a lovely café in Knaresborough they called the Blue Bell Café. It must have been a very hot day and I had eleven cups of tea for fourpence, I bet you could have pricked me with a pin.

We used to go camping on Friday night to Primrose Valley and back Sunday, the boys in one tent and the girls in another. We borrowed blankets and things for about tuppence, and sixpence for the tent. There were no sleeping bags, you made your own, I remember sewing one up. And there were enormous ground sheets, you got them for a shilling. One day some men had been fishing and they had a bucket full of whitings they'd just caught and didn't want, so 'Would you like them?'

I says, 'Can a duck swim?' We ran to where the bucket was and they were that fresh, talk about 'your dinner is assured', they were lovely. It was all right because we took our own primus stoves.

From Primrose Valley we'd walk all the way to Filey, right along the end of the Brig, about ten miles. And I ate a whole loaf of bread with nothing on it, I can't remember ever being so hungry. One of our lads had been to Blackpool and he knew we were at Primrose Valley and he came and joined us in a day, coast to coast. I've never done that, it would have been about 140 miles rough. A mere bagatelle!

There were church services, one at Coxwold, what they call the cyclist's Sunday. We'd go every year to this service, and once it'd been pouring down all night and they played steam with me at home, thought I was mad. Well I *was* mad, 'cos we only got to Skelton and we couldn't cross the road for two foot of water! And we hadn't got much further, to Shipton, and there was another flood across the road and we got wet again. We got to Coxwold eventually, too wet to go to church. But I knew the landlady in the Fauconberg Arms and we went in there, and I went to church in her husband's socks and somebody else's slippers.

Mrs C., born 1909

An Olympic Hero

Harold Porter with the cup won for York Harriers, 1922.

My cousin Noel and myself were quite close as teenagers and I used to spend a lot of time at his house in Upper Price Street in the late '40s and early '50s. He lived with his grandad and his mother and father, Agnes and Harold Porter. Harold was a clerk at the Electricity Board, a quiet unassuming chap of a nervous disposition, who never talked much about his past life. One day my dad told me that uncle Harold got a bronze medal in the 1924 Paris Olympic Games, when he ran against Paavo Nurmi, the flying Finn. I tended to look at uncle Harold in a different light after that but I never asked him about his running prowess and it was later in life that I decided to look into his background. I discovered that he had in fact won a silver medal in the

Harold Porter in second place running with York Harriers, 1923.

York Harriers two mile team, Harold Porter is seated on the left, 1923.

Programme for the Paris Olympics, 1924.

800 metre relay race (now no longer an Olympic event), perhaps the greatest achievement of any York athlete.

He was a national athlete, running for Great Britain in a match against the USA before a crowd of 25,000 at Stamford Bridge, London, the week following the Olympic Games. In the same year he won the Yorkshire four mile, one mile and half mile championships in one week in August and took part in an international event in Glasgow in the same month. He retired from running when he was twenty-four, which was young for a middle distance runner, because he said it was getting too much. They were amateurs in those days and he had a job. He ran during his holidays and at weekends and evenings, they didn't give him time off work. Perhaps the success of the charismatic athletes like Harold Abrahams and Eric Liddell in the same year took the limelight away from one of York's forgotten heroes.

Mike Race, born 1938

Ordinary Guy

He used to go about his job, just an ordinary guy. It wasn't like it is now, if it had been in this day and age, he would have been a world beater. It was an amateur sport in them days. All dad got was a few little prizes, they certainly didn't get any money for it. He ran for York Harriers, started at seventeen, in 1920. He had his twenty-first birthday while he was in Paris. He told us about the good times, and he met a lot of people including the Prince of Wales. But he never used to talk about it much at all.

Noel Porter, born 1938

Albert Allison Keech, known as Bert, was born in 1906 and died in 1954. He was well known in York in many circles, especially in sport.

A Man of Many Sports

The Bootham and District Bowling Club played opposite the Minster. Apart from bowls, he represented York at soccer, rugby union, rugby league and rowing. And he was table tennis

Harold Porter in Olympic outfit in 1924.

Bootham Bowling Club, August 1950. Australia *v.* Yorkshire; Australia won 125-116.

champion of York for three years. He also played cricket and hockey, and billiards and snooker. Bert was a big man, he got to twenty-five stones. He used to take me to all the race meetings: I've been to Ascot. And once we were on a bowling tour of Scotland, and they finished on the Friday and he said, 'Edith there's some races at Hamilton Park.' Oh I can picture it now, such a pretty little course. He went right through the card; he backed six winners. It paid all expenses plus. Do you know, no bookmaker in York would take his bets, 'cos he won too much money.

Edith Keech, born 1913

But it was bowls which brought Bert the most fame, and he even went to America, winning the Florida pairs.

Magnetic Personality

Bert was a magnetic personality. You knew who he was. He was an established international. He'd played for York Wednesdays in 1937 as goalie, and he kicked the ball the full length of the field, it was a penalty, from one goal right into the far goal. Bert beat his father the first time he won the rinks. He was good from an early age. I remember when Bert went with the England team to Florida in 1947 and him sending me dad a card from America and that was certainly the only foreign postcard that came to our house in Layerthorpe for many years.

Bootham bowling rink (group of four) in 1926. Bert Keech stands on the right.

78

As a young lad if I occasionally went up to Glen Garth, he might be playing a match there and I remember him coming one night and he always had a big car and a big leather square case with all his gear in, whereas most normal people went to play bowls on their bikes and they had a couple of woods in a net strung over their handlebars and me dad used to wear his flat bowling shoes on his bike. Bert had been the singles champion in 1945 and he'd won a lot of other things. And he had great big woods, bigger than most. In those days they were made of a hard wood that came from the West Indies and one set of four was made from one piece.

David Poole, born 1940

Bert Keech and son in 1953, a year before his death.

Twenty-one Up

I joined the boys' club in Redeness Street off Layerthorpe about 1951 and table tennis was one of the main sports. They'd had a team in the York league for many years but it tended to be older lads that played. In 1952 they'd just got a new leader and they entered a team in the junior division of the York and District League and I started playing and I was winning more than half the games when I was twelve. By the time I was fourteen we entered the men's league as well so at that point we were playing against adult clubs like the Railway Institute, and RAF stations, with servicemen who were there for two or three years. There was an article in the paper at that time about a bigwig who was in command of sport in the RAF, who

encouraged people who were good at table tennis to say so when they were called up for national service. If you were good at football, the Army pinched you but sports like table tennis, the RAF did. At one time in the early '50s we had two Scottish international table tennis players, one at Church Fenton and the other at Linton. There was about five divisions of ten, and there was three men in a team. You all played each other at singles, and any two of you played a double at the end so there were ten matches. It was just right for the time available 'cos you'd start at half past seven and a normal match would go on until ten.

When I started work for the council,

York Men's Table Tennis Team, January 1966. At the Railway Institute, from left to right: Billy Hulmes, Dennis Norburn, Francis Gregoire, David Poole.

the union NALGO had had a team for years and I went to play for them. We played in the Grange dining-hall on Huntington Road, the old workhouse. It was a wood block floor and we had a lighting set above, three decent-sized bulbs in a row over the table.

The league had started in 1927 and table tennis really wasn't organized nationally before then. Some enthusiasts had set up a team in Tang Hall and before they moved to Tang Hall Hotel, they played in the bedroom of one of the members in a council house in Melrosegate. I think it was a three-bedroomed house and I don't know how many kids they had. Somebody once said that they took the door knob off to make more room. They were one of the early ones, and pre-war there were church groups and the YMCA were quite active.

Each year they ran championships.

Men's singles, women's singles and doubles. The junior singles was for under eighteen. I won it in 1955 when I was fourteen. The lad who I beat was seventeen, he'd had a lot more experience and I was obviously the underdog and I surprised myself when I beat him. In 1958 I won the junior singles again. In 1957 I got chosen for the county junior team. I was playing for the York league but the county team was made up of three boys and a girl and it was selected from all the leagues in Yorkshire. We played against Cheshire and Lancashire and were unbeaten, and then we played the winners of the southern Junior League, Middlesex, and got beaten at that point.

I moved into the York men's first team when I was seventeen. The season started late September and ran until Easter. They often staged the championships in the Railway Institute and they had ten tables set up in a row. I was a defender and I had to work hard at it. Some people were naturals but others had to slog it out. I had some tremendously long matches.

In 1958, I also won men's singles as well as the junior singles on the same night. I was seventeen and it was the first time it had been done – and the first time any junior had won the men's singles. But I didn't get to the county team again because I was a defender. I could beat a player the first time but after that, they'd know my game and could often beat me.

In the mid to late '50s the pub closing time was half past ten and if I was in the middle of a long match at the Grange, the others used to get a bit annoyed because you could nip on your bikes through the ground of the City Hospital attached to the Grange and pop into the Punch Bowl on Lowther Street and get a pint before they closed. But if I was over-running, and I was more bothered about winning than having a pint, I would stick it out. As I got older I lost a bit of competitive edge and I would rather have had a pint than stick there for another half hour.

I started playing bowls when I was twenty and once the table tennis season had finished in early April you were ready for a change. My dad played for Layerthorpe bowling club at Glen Gardens and I used to go up on summer nights watching and I started about 1959. I won the county junior singles championship in 1964 and the table tennis county juniors in 1959. No-one else has done it in both bowls and table tennis. I entered the York

singles competition and won it in 1968. I won the Bert Keech singles trophy in 1970 and the county pairs in 1967 and we won the York rinks (four men) title in 1966 and were runners-up in the pairs in 1969. What is attractive about bowls is that it is relatively cheap, it's leisurely, relaxing and you don't have to stay out all that long. You can turn up at quarter to seven and get a full game in by nine.

David Poole, born 1940

York City Football

I was born in 1912. I went to Acomb council school and we hadn't a football team or even a playing field but we played in the school yard with a tennis ball. Then the headmaster said, 'Can you pick a team to play Poppleton Road old boys? They've won everything.' I picked a team and we drew, so Cyril Baxter picked four of us from our school for a trial with York City Boys' and he gradually whittled us down to one so I got selected. We had a pretty good run but we got knocked out at Grimsby in the cup. In that team there were six of them went to be internationals. Then I got selected for Yorkshire boys' team and I got picked for England boys' team in the same season and captained them against Scotland. I started in a sixteen-eighteen team when I was only fourteen and it was called Acomb Carr Lane. I became quite strong and I tackled hard. I was asked by one of the directors Mr Pratt out of Holgate Road for a trial with York City. I wasn't the age to sign on so I had to wait, it was fifteen, and the very date it was my birthday they signed me on to York City. I started on about £3 a week. I had a job as an instrument maker for British Rail and with that money and the money for York City, I was better off than a full-time professional who only got £7 a week. It's a precarious game is soccer and I kept me job.

I played in the Yorkshire League team reserves. They were nearly all local lads. It was a real good side. In 1932 we moved to Bootham Crescent. The first manager at York City was brilliant, Jock Collier, he put York on the map, he'd get some lovely players. Spud Murphy was the trainer and we bought two players from Newcastle –

Tommy MacDonald and Joe Harris. They wore bowler hats in them days and it tickled me to see them come down in bowler hats but they were good players because they played in the first division all the time. We used to get treated all the time by a gentleman called Mr Stanley for injuries. Nowadays if they have a pulled hamstring they're off for months and he'd just put heat on us and paint across our legs and he could get us ready in a fortnight. I know it's a lot faster the game nowadays, the boots are lighter and instead of having to run at a ball, they can just flick it. The old balls used to weigh a ton and mud used to cling, and your great boots,

York City Football team, complete with mascot (Mr York), in 1936. From left to right, the players are: Claude Barrett, Ted Hathway, Dick Duckworth, Ted Wass, Malcolm Comrie, -?-, Norman Wharton (goalie), Jim Hughes, Jack Pinder, Peter Spooner, -?-.

Jack Pinder at work at the railway, *c.* 1940.

sometimes you thought you had the roller behind you. We had a good cup run when I played, we had some happy days, they were always a well run club, always in the black.

In the '30s there were only two of us, Reg Baines and myself, and the rest were full-time professionals. It was a tougher game. My first game was against Stockport county. We beat them 2-0. I think everybody's a bit nervous but as soon as you go out on the field you forget that. We went to Huddersfield and I played in front of 58,000 and 10,000 out on a hill watching outside and it didn't bother me – we drew with them.

Our boss at work was Mr Trapps and we had a good crew and every night I used to get them singing *The Old Rugged Cross* ten minutes before we went home. When we were going away training I went up to the window and said, 'Can I have a week off to go training?' 'Aye all right lad, it'll be a change from *The Old Rugged Cross* for a week'.

In my day there was no bad

Girls' gymnastics at Rowntrees, 1930s.

language, it was lovely, just the chap from the Red Cross sat with two policemen each match. I don't remember anything bad at all. I've enjoyed it. I wasn't a brilliant scholar but I was always spoiled at school because I was playing for England boys. The headmaster used to give me half a crown every time I went away to play. And when he retired, and every year when I got earning money, I used to take a big box of cigars round to give back what he'd given to me at school. After about five years he said, 'Jack I'll have to tell you, I don't smoke. My son smokes them. But thank you for your kind thought'.

Jack Pinder, born 1912

Girls' Gymnastics

They used to have gymnastics twice a week at Rowntrees. The boys and the girls enjoyed it and it gave us time off work. The company believed that 'a healthy body means a healthy mind'.

Nell McTurk (neé Wildon), born 1896

CHAPTER 6

The church

Methodist meeting in Skeldergate, *c.* 1920.

The church had a much stronger influence in the 1920s than it does today. For many people, it also represented a large part of their social life.

Wesley Sunday School

We went to Wesley Sunday school. It was the one which my father went to and my grandfather had a lot to do with. The children went until they were a certain age then seemed to drift away. They asked if he could start a class for the older ones, and it absolutely took off and it could sometimes have as many as three or four hundred there every Sunday afternoon. So they had to move from Wesley because it wasn't big enough and they started the Old Priory Adult School. It was quite a York thing, they were known as 'Bob Kay's lambs'.

Hilda Beaumont, born 1904

Signing The Pledge

At the Band of Hope they used to teach us little rhymes to sing like 'My drink is water bright from the crystal spring'. They got all the children to sign the pledge at an early age. I should be six or seven and you really didn't understand what you were signing. But there was an awful lot of drunkenness. I can remember seeing children standing outside the pubs with no shoes or stockings on, waiting for parents to come out. The pubs were open all day and probably the children were hungry and gone to look for their parents. My mother was teetotal and

belonged to the British Women's Temperance Union. They wore a little white ribbon brooch like a lover's knot, only in white, and it was to try and encourage women not to go the same way as some of their husbands. At the Band of Hope we had meetings where we were taught on a magic lantern the evils of drink.

Mrs S. H., born 1904

The Band of Hope Outing

We belonged to the Band of Hope and in the summer we'd go for an outing. This gentleman had a flat cart and we'd all assemble to go on it. It was pulled by one of the big shire horses and it was beautifully got up, ribbons and brasses and all the rest. And the cart of course being cleaned and washed, they put straw on. The girls had to sit in the middle and the boys could sit with their legs dangling all the way round. They thought that was marvellous, and we used to go as far as the Homestead at Clifton and we thought we'd reached the other end of the earth, because very few of us ever went on holidays.

Mrs S. H., born 1904

The Salvation Army

I worked on a farm in Huntington and one Sunday night the farmer and his wife and the bairns were going out to tea which was rare. He says, 'You can finish earlier tonight and go where you want', so I had a walk into York and I saw all the Salvation Army going in at

Band of Hope Gala, 1906.

the gate. I was curious and a chap come across and says, 'Are you coming into the service?' I said, 'No these are the only clothes I've got on'. I'd just cleaned t' pigs out. He says, 'Come on, you'll be all right'. It was harvest time at the Salvation Army and it was lovely, decorated out with fruit. They spoke of the prodigal son and that was me, he was talking to me.

I kept going and the farmer said, 'If you're not in by nine o'clock, the gate will be shut', and I've run down that lane and it's been striking nine by Huntington church clock and I got to the gate and it had shut and the light's gone off. I'd go in the cowhouse and sleep on the hay, I wouldn't sleep on straw because of the rats. Then I took up an instrument, the bass tuba and I only had a sheet with three scales on. I persevered and kept doing it, it was gone ten some nights.

When I was eighteen I left the farm and got started at Blundy Clark's, shovelling coal. After a year I went into the Army, and the Salvation Army bandmaster was losing a few of the older ones so he took some new ones on. When I got called up, I still played. Everywhere we went we used to make ourselves known, the Salvation Army, and they were very good to us. We played in different bands and the better the band the more we learnt, and I finished up in the staff band in the military when the war finished.

Me and the wife used to sing duets in the pubs, take our bikes to the Groves and Walmgate and sing, *The Old Rugged Cross* and sell the *War Cry*. People had a lot of respect for the Salvation Army. They used to say, 'Watch your language'. I still played in the Salvation Army band, and later I played with the railway band at garden fetes and parks. My wife's auntie was put in the workhouse and she was in for donkey's years until they released her. She got a flat and it's the Salvation Army that's kept her sane. I'll allus be indebted to them.

George Bye, born 1923

Albion Street Mission

I was brought up a Methodist and attended the Wesley mission on Skeldergate, at the corner of Queen's Staith road. I found them very supportive. They were very homely, it was down-to-earth Christianity. They used to have evening services out in the middle of Albion Street or Beedham's Court. You achieved everything if you

Doris Lonsdale, 1925.

did 104 attendances, morning and afternoon for 52 weeks in the year. Many a book I had – a prize for over 100 attendances. I was keenly interested, I thought they were lovely people, they were there to help. A simple service – to me it's sincerity. I'm not one for repeating religious idiom. I'm still a Methodist at heart. On Christmas Eve they used to come round carol singing. I was awakened and would go to the window, it was getting on for twelve o'clock. My father would shout down to them, 'Before you go everybody, and it's lovely to have had you, will you sing one more chorus of *O come all ye who are faithful*? And they did.

Syd Heppell, born 1921

Keeping The Commandments

We went to St Maurice's. After the First World War we all had to take a penny to school and it was for a Union Jack. They put a screen in the church as a memorial for the lads who'd been to Bedern school and killed in the war. The vicar at the church wasn't a very good preacher but he was very good at going to visit anybody that was ill in the hospital, because he lived near it. We were taught the ten commandments and I always remember me mother saying to us as we grew up that if you live by the ten commandments, you won't go far wrong and that is really true. Nowadays life is just taken with no thought. I think the wars have done this.

Doris Lonsdale, born 1907

Exhibition Buildings.

Church Was My Life

Church was really me life. I went to Sunday school and straight into church on the morning, go home and have me dinner and then Sunday school again and then church with me mother at night. I went to the YPU, the Young People's Union. We went to St Barnabas on Leeman Road and when we were children, on Saturday afternoons it was watching weddings. We'd wait for the bride to go in and when she came out, we'd run like billy-o to the chapel and they'd always put pennies over the fire and throw them out and they were red hot, and those that you could hold you kept.

Vera Thomlinson, born 1916

Songs at The Band of Hope

On Friday night I had to go to the Band of Hope in Exhibition Buildings, which is now the Art Gallery. We had to give our names in either to sing or recite or read and I'd put my name down the Friday before and I'd forgotten. I'd just been listening to the tingalarie, the barrel organ, outside so I started to sing a common song that was all the go and I sang it with my hand on my hip taking off the music halls, and the chief man said, 'No Nell that'll do nicely, we don't sing those kind of songs at the Band of Hope'. We used to sing *Water is Best* and *Give said the little stream, give oh give*. When I worked at Rowntrees years later, he was our head man, and he reminded me about that.

Nell McTurk (née Wildon), born 1896

Band of Hope fancy dress display, *c.* 1909. Nell Wildon is on the back row, third from left, in black hat and Welsh costume. Her sister Gertie Wildon is also on the back row, on the far left.

Girls' Friendly Society

Together with a friend, I founded a Girls' Friendly Society branch at St Thomas with St Maurice church about 1947. We had our ups and downs but we always seemed to come through after prayer and hard work. We had a varied programme – play and instruction, and working at various handicrafts which were often towards annual competitions held between the different branches in the diocese. A special day was arranged for the branches to meet for awards, tea and a service. We tried to help with various interests of the parish, like the annual gift day or autumn fair. I can remember the branch opening a bazaar, the theme was the rainbow, and the girls all dressed in coloured dresses. We were fortunate one year that our branch was chosen to send a member to one of the royal garden parties which was a great honour. Over the years we have taken part in many birthdays of the GFS celebrated in various cathedrals – Coventry, Westminster Abbey and the 100th birthday at York Minster. I remember the members going to London for one celebration and sleeping in the underground shelters on Clapham Common, just after the last war, and another visit to London with an invitation to have tea in the grounds of Lambeth Palace. The branch closed down but our banner still remains in church as a reminder of many happy and successful years.

Norah Arnot

CHAPTER 7

Two world wars

Vine Street victory party, 1918.

The First World War

A Typist in The Forces

In the First World War, I went in the forces as a shorthand typist. I did shorthand classes on a night at Castlegate school and I liked typing. In 1917 I was about nineteen and we was in Fossgate, over the top of Stubbs the ironmongers, then we went to Tadcaster in a camp at Bramham Moor. I enjoyed it, it was a change. We had to sleep in Army huts, about twenty in one.

Myrtle Hardisty, born 1898

George Gledhill, 1918. He served in the Fifth battalion of the West Yorkshire Regiment, in France.

Scouts Help the War Effort

War broke out on August 4th 1914, and I remember going to school after the bank holiday and we hadn't got a school. I was fourteen and in the boy scouts. We were all lined up and marched off to go to the military establishments in and around York. There was quite a number of messengers and general dogsbodies, carrying letters or going to the barracks and getting rations for the troops. My first posting was to the Territorial Association whose office was in St Leonard's. Brigadier General Mannings was in command. Before long I was moved off to York castle where there were two entrances. One was a drive-in entry to get a coach through, facing the law courts, and that was the prison or detention barracks, primarily for detention of troops who got into trouble getting drunk or fighting. There was also another part where they had German prisoners. The commander there was Major Hattle, a very nice chap, he had been in the Zulu wars. He taught me how to shoot on a 25 yard range with ordinary service rifles, they used to take smaller bullets. He got very cross with me one day because I had the thing already shooting when he was on the range.

George Thomas, born 1901

Horses And Mules

I was nearly four years over there on the Somme and Ypres. My job was with horses and mules, getting rations up to the lads in the trenches. On the top all the time, but I never got a scratch. I remember coming on leave after being

Taking the King's shilling in front of Exhibition Buildings (now the York Art Gallery), 1914.

there nine months. I had a pair of mules which I loved and I wanted to get back to them and instead of being able to, I fell ill at home and never saw 'em again. I'd got right attached to that pair of mules. I finished up as a Lance Jack, a Lance Corporal.

George Gledhill, born 1894

The King's Shilling

I was called up when I was eighteen and had to report to Bootham and he gave me this King's shilling and marched me to the infantry barracks at Fulford Road. The idea is that you got the King's shilling and you'd been accepted. The following day I went back and they gave me a uniform and packed me off to Pontefract.

I was in the Durham Light Infantry and I was sent abroad on the Belgian front at Ypres. I was in this front line and

one of the chaps says to me, 'Lend me your watch and I'll know what time to wake you up for your stint', but instead of getting me watch back, I never saw him again. We went over the top for the first three days and I've an idea that there was a hundred killed then and we was relieved at night and taken out of the line then taken back and the result was that before the 11 November 1918 we had advanced about thirty miles.

Edwin Lofthouse, born 1899

War Service

My eldest sister, Gertie, had lost her fiancé in the Boer War. She never married. In the First World War she went to help at the station with the canteen for soldiers and sailors and she worked there for some time.

Nell McTurk, born 1896

93

War Service.

November, 1915, to May, 1919.

War service at York station during the First World War. Gertie Wildon is at the back, sixth from right, behind the table.

Street Parties

The day peace was declared in 1918, I was only fifteen, but got to know that something was going on and it came out at eleven o'clock. Our pub was full – the yard, outside, they were everywhere. Then a customer brought some jumping crackers in. You can imagine the pandemonium.

Mabel Wilson, born 1903

The Second World War

Terry's Aircraft Production

Hills from Manchester came during the war and took so much of Terry's over and I was working on aircraft propellers. I ended up being in charge of the department.

York was full of air force of every nationality. The Free French were at Elvington and there was Dutch and Poles who were very gentlemanly, clicked their heels and made you feel you was somebody. There was just tiny little star lights on the roads but nothing in the streets, everywhere was pitch black, yet you could walk about quite freely and you never thought about anybody attacking you. When I used to be on nights at Hills, we did three shifts, I've come home at all sorts of hours on me bike and it never entered your head that you were in any danger, and the town was choc-a-bloc with forces. It was a very different world altogether.

Where Lister's electrical shop is on

Poppleton Road, for years and years it was a fruit shop and Wilf Exelby kept it. If a whisper got out that Wilf had tomatoes, mothers were queueing from half past seven until Wilf opened at nine. Or if there was oranges, mother used to dash and queue. You used to get six pennyworth of meat, and it's rather amazing, the butchers could cut exactly six pennyworth. But we were all well fed and had a staple diet.

One of the girls at Hills had a brother-in-law on the Gold Coast and he came over on leave and brought some little Canary bananas, very small and very sweet, and she gave me two. Ooh, it was an absolute luxury. And I've never known two bananas make so many sandwiches in me life. Children that were born during the war, they didn't know what a banana was.

Winnie Mothersdale, born 1912

The First Woman Driver

During the war I used to be the porter on the station platform. There was no signs those days to tell you where anything was going, on account of if an invasion came. So we all had to know exactly which train was going where. Trains would come in wi' t' wounded soldiers and they were all shouting to you and you were getting 'em teas. And they used to come through the station, mebbe going up to Newcastle and there were hardly any lights in those days, and I found a lady's fur coat, she'd left it on a train. The stationmaster asked me if I would like anything (for finding it) and I said, 'If ever there's any women drivers, yes'.

And I would be t' first woman driver at York, because they taught me to drive. And when they bombed York, they were definitely after the railway, and they come right over the convent and killed some nuns. Next morning we had to go to work to our vans. No work, because everything was bombed, but they put a bag in the back of me van and a policeman come to sit at side of me and he said, 'You're going to Kent Street love. You don't know what's in the bag?' I says, 'No'. Well it was the body of the man who was killed in the railway station, Milner they called him. I took it to the mortuary in Kent Street which was the old cattle market and the policeman said, 'Don't come in and look'. But me curiosity overcame me and I did go in and all the bodies were laid out, families; mother and father and children, and their few belongings.

Eileen Brow, born 1914

The ATS

I said if I can go into the ATS, I can be attached to the Ordnance as a clerk then I can have a home posting. But I had to go to Harrogate for three weeks' training, doing square bashing and getting your uniforms. Then I was outside Nottingham on an RAOC clerk's course. I passed it and you got a posting after six weeks and I was at Chilwell, the biggest RAOC depot in England. I got a home posting eventually, after two and a half years! I was attached to the Ordnance Depot in York, and it was only at the top of the street. When the war was over they made it one of the demob centres in

Nancy Dawson, second from right, in the ATS in Ordnance Lane, 1946.

1946. But I enjoyed it in the forces, I really did.

Nancy Dawson, born 1922

Bombed Out

I was born in 1933. In those days you had an Anderson shelter, a corrugated iron thing buried in the back garden. Me dad had a terraced house, which had a backyard in Lavender Grove and he also made the cupboard under the stairs into our shelter. During that night in April 1942 sirens went off and he took us into the yard to see all Clifton Ings on fire, incendiary bombs all over, it was all lit up. You could see the bombs dropping but over to the left, a plane came over the top of the allotments, which are still there at the back of Lavender Grove, and started machine gunning the railway. He said, 'Right, it's time to get inside' and as we got into the shelter it went 'bang' and

that was it. It actually landed, not in the middle of the street, nearer to the semi-detached than the terraced ones, and just blew the whole lot down. The whole front of the house came in, the roof, the back walls, everything. And that's when me dad carried us out of the shelter, me sister under one arm, me under the other. I'll never forget that, standing in the back yard and seeing the house disappear. We were sent to a house on Boroughbridge Road, which was the collecting point for everybody which had been bombed out, where they issued you with clothes. Me mum and dad got a couple of blankets and tins of food, and I was given a monopoly set to play with. It was American. You play in dollars, not in pounds.

It used to be fun in one sense at school when you were putting your gas masks on. You didn't think of it as being horrible, it was just fun – until you get bombed out. Then it's totally different, you've nowhere to live, you've lost all your toys. The only things that really survived were me dad's grandmother clock, and all the Christmas tree decorations – there wasn't one of those broken, and they were in a box in a wardrobe in the front bedroom, which had disappeared!

And I remember me mother said, 'You won't be going to school tomorrow, look at your school.' And all there was, was a chimney stack and a big hole right in the centre. I never went to Poppleton Road school again. Because of the length of time to repair it, I was sent to finish my education to Scarcroft School.

Peter Binns, born 1933

Clifton Aerodrome

The activities at Clifton Aerodrome started in 1936 under the auspices of the Yorkshire Aviation Services. In September 1939 the aerodrome was taken over by Linton-on-Ouse and became a satellite of Linton. It was mainly used in the early part for Army co-operation using Lysander aircraft. Later, Linton used it as an emergency landing ground and eventually it became a servicing aerodrome for Halifax four-engined bombers. The two large hangars that are now used as grain stores were the two main hangars used for the repair of damaged Halifax aircraft. They also used to bring them back from the Middle East to be de-sanded, because the main planes got clogged with sand, they were brought back to be made serviceable. Having a family in York, I made use of the aerodrome on two or three occasions. I was allowed to fly from my RAF aerodrome to York to visit my wife in her nursing home and the second time was after the large air raid when the Germans came over to the cathedral towns. My father's shop in Bootham was flattened

Poppleton Road School after the Blitz, April 1942.

Food salvage in Walney Road, Heworth during the Second World War.

and they asked if I would come to give him a hand. He had a glass and china shop, and that's a bit vulnerable to bombing raids and there was very little left of the shop at all. There was a glass showcase that was completely smashed apart from one shelf and in the corner there was a Royal Doulton figure of Mr Churchill and it was still there.

Richard Harwood, born 1913

Waste Collection

During the war we started up a system of collecting kitchen waste from houses and took it down to our yard and put it in three digesters and cooked this stuff up to make it safe to serve to animals and sold it to pig dealers. We also collected waste paper and baled that and sold it, and collected tins and sold

them and that worked really well.

Charles Minter, born 1897

Home Guard

I passed all me exams for the Home Guard, maps, rifle shooting and machine guns. I got all me certificates. There was some in the Home Guard and some on fire watching, ARP. There were so many fire watchers in the village and I used to go out and if there was a fire there, take extinguishers. You had to have no light showing through your windows. They'd all go to the search light unit once a fortnight in turn, stay all night and if they had a warning gone, you had to go and wake the area Home Guard up. Once a fortnight you got a rest 'cos you were working every day as well. We had a meeting about three times a

98

week and church parade once a month. You had mock battles, one platoon against another. I was in reserved occupation on the farm, they couldn't be called up, essential for growing food. We still got our rations and we got an extra two ounce of cheese for farm workers. We always had plenty of food with a pig, a cow and plenty of hens.

Jack Smith, born 1910

Fleet Air Arm

I lived in Clifton. I was four when the war began and I remember it being used as a military aerodrome and the big planes coming in and crews being billeted with people in the locality. We had numerous young men billeted with us because we had a spare room. I think my mother said she was paid something like three and sixpence a night. These young men were full of life, eighteen, ninteen year olds and I remember their uniform because we had Fleet Air men. They had a darker uniform than the RAF, it was more a navy blue and I used to put their caps on and they had the most beautiful badge on the front, like a crown, padded and scarlet with gold wire over the top. They were awfully nice to me, saying, 'I've got a sister just like you'. If I'd been ten years older I think I would have had much more fun. Being about eight, I thoroughly enjoyed them and I remember we had one very nice young man whose great friend was billeted just down the road with my friend's parents and he went to Doncaster as a favour to somebody and they ran into a factory chimney and he was killed. He'd just got married and his wife was a teacher at the local school. I gave him a tiny

Home Guard at Alne, with Jack Smith.

Ash Street victory party, 1945.

teddy bear, about four inches long and it had a little orange waistcoat with knotted buttons and he called it Plumpy and he had it in his aircraft and in exchange he gave me *The Wind in the Willows*. I've still got it and inside it says, 'In exchange for Plumpy who I'm sure was a friend of Pooh and the people in this book'.

The war was terrible but children accept things don't they? It was just the way the world was. And we used to play war games, 'Bang bang you're dead', and fall down and then get up and run about. I do remember clearly John who lived in Malton Way off Shipton Road came round and said, 'The war's over'. I said, 'Go on, I don't believe you'. He said, 'I know it is 'cos my mum's crying'. And I couldn't wait to see bunting in the street. I remember flags being put out and my granny taking me down Rawcliffe Lane to see the houses lit up in the dark. I was so used to black-out, I thought it was like

fairy lights, I was so thrilled with it, all the windows had different coloured curtains. I thought it was wonderful.

Gwyneth Hopper, born 1935

The Night Of The Raid

On the night of the raid when the sirens sounded, you only got a warning on the phone, and when I went over Ouse Bridge I could see there was a light there – they were restoring the Guildhall at that time but never got finished. We had the Archbishop lined up to open it and the bomb dropped and set it on fire and it was spreading fast. We got the drawings, as much as we could out of the drawing office. One of my assistants and me went through my office into this committee room and the door slammed behind us and we couldn't get back. We saw the blaze and we put tin hats on and made a run for it right across to my office. We got molten lead on our hats and backs but we didn't get hurt. The fire brigade came and the roof burnt. After the raid, General Bartholomew came along and I went out with the superintendent of works to see the damage near the Mansion House and we went down into Leeman Road where they got a crater in the middle of the crossroads. When we got there, there was this party on the other side of the road, with the Princess Royal. So I went over and they introduced me to the Princess Royal and he said, 'This is the City Engineer, he gets on with the job and argues the point afterwards'.

Charles Minter, born 1897

The Parachute Regiment

I was born in St Saviour's Place in 1923. I went in 1941 to the West Yorkshire Regiment. I tried to get into the Navy but you had more sailors than ships them days. I stayed in the Army until '47. I did special commando training and transferred straight to the parachute regiment – eight weeks training, parachute jumps and things like forced marches and fitness.

We dropped at the D-Day landings at Caan from Dakotas. It was pretty intense because we were only supposed to be there for two days, they expected them getting through, but they didn't. It took them a lot longer to get up from the beachheads with the casualties they had. We were on the crossroads stopping the reinforcements from getting through to the Germans that were protecting the

beachhead. We were in Normandy probably over a month. Once the beachhead got the momentum, they wanted us back to train and we reformed into the Parachute Division with Boy Browning that went over to Arnhem with the Tenth Battalion.

We all knew where we were going and what we were doing, but on the ground we didn't know what we were up against. The Germans had congregated the remnants of their Panzer divisions and were reorganizing. So we parachuted into that sort of area where you were trying to hit heavy armoured vehicles with light machine guns. In the narrow streets around Arnhem you had men jumping out of a window and shoving a hand grenade through a slit in the tank and getting off as quick as they could, that was the only thing you had. It was inevitable in the end, we had to withdraw. Ammunition, food, water, was in very short supply. We'd eat a lot of apples from the orchards. But the people didn't have food to give you. They were helpful to start off, but when they saw that things were going against us they couldn't be too helpful because the danger of reprisals was very high.

I got shrapnel wounds, just light stuff, but it never knocked me out too much, even a bullet through the top of the leg went through one side and out the other through the flesh. It didn't hit the bone. There weren't enough boats to take people across the Rhine so we had to swim out there, the main body came out with what boats they could. It was strong currents and very cold water and when you hit the other bank, you were very exposed. But the Germans didn't fire at us. It was probably soldier pride or something. Being soldiers and infantrymen they thought that you'd got that far and good luck.

There was odd times, you'd get that feeling, when you're in a tight corner, 'What am I doing here?' But as soon as a bit of action comes up you forget everything. You've got to survive to go back to your regiment, so you think about living. Then the adrenalin takes over. The worst time is the waiting.

The time I had adjusting was when I came out of the Army. You had nothing to bother about, the framework was all built in around you, and you were used to that. But you came back to a quiet life without the comradeship of the men around you, and it's very hard to settle down.

Sometimes you can wake up with a sweat in the middle of the night and relive some of it. You may do it two or three times a month, or you might go six months without, but it's always there. Sometimes a young person might say,

'Can't you forget the war?' It's easy for them to say it, but you can never forget, because the subconscious mind is better then any computer.

Early on I lost some close friends, but after that I had many friends but I never got too close, especially when I got sergeant's stripes, because you'd be the one that had to write to the family. They were good friends, good comrades, but I didn't want to know anything about their backgrounds. You don't only live together, you live or die together, because you rely on each other that much.

John Waite, born 1923

The Burma Star

My mother joined the Women's Auxiliary Service Burma, it was attached to the 14th Army, Sir William

Parade of Burma Star Association veterans in Parliament Street, Vivian Stuart is the only woman, 1950s.

Slim was in charge. She was devoted to the Burma Star Association and I think she set it all up. She was the only woman in York, I don't think there were many. Mother went to the Burma Star Association meetings in London and she'd made friends with a Japanese person who's still alive, must be eighty-something and he came over to the Burma Star to ask for forgiveness and he was terribly pleased because she bore no grudge to the Japanese. His job was nothing to do with war crimes, it was just to do with radio or newspapers but he met Lord Louis Mountbatten and was always grateful because they became friends. Mother went to all the meetings and would say, 'Lord Louis shook my hand, I'm never going to wash it again'.

Jenny Gooch, born 1936

An Absolute Objector

Born in 1915 and brought up during the aftermath of the terrible first war, it made a vivid impression on me to see ex-servicemen, maimed and unemployed, begging in the streets of York trying to make a meagre living. I still remember one regular specimen who used to play records on a large gramophone and after a shower of rain when the streets were quiet, the silence was suddenly broken by the strains of *Roses of Picardy* rendered on a cornet by another maimed ex-soldier. It seemed unthinkable to me to have any more wars.

I was a pacifist right from the time I went to Scarcroft Road council school from 1919 to 1929, leaving at the age of fourteen. The strict method of teaching was 'come out the boy that doesn't know', if you got your sums wrong or made a spelling mistake, you got the cane. Violence. At a very early age I got the idea that it was wrong to have violence inflicted upon you and it was also wrong to inflict violence on other people and that's perhaps how it was deeply ingrained in me not to take part in war. I thought if there was another war, I would take no part in it, I would become a conscientious objector. It was quite a few years later that the Second World War broke out.

As far as was humanly possible, I did nothing at all to help the war machine. I registered as a CO claiming absolute exemption. The form was sent to Leeds at a tribunal in 1940. I felt that it was mentally, morally and psychologically impossible to accept any decision of the court that did not allow me exemption. I had to appear in front of Judge Stewart who was notorious for making remarks about 'conchies' being cowards. He did offer me hospital work or work on the land alternatively to joining the Army.

But it was an important principle for the absolute conscientious objector – they would not accept any condition of getting out of military service. There was an appeal held in York and the answer was 'We cannot allow this man to go scot free'. I had to prove that I was not a coward and face the consequences – of going to prison. On 11 September 1941, I was sentenced to six months in prison and a fine of £25. If I didn't pay the fine, I would get another three months.

PC Simpson took me to York station and we got on the train, a one-way ticket for me, to Leeds and I got my first taste of prison in Armley Jail. The sentence was 'with hard labour' and you had the first fortnight in a cell in solitary

Ron Jeffrey in 1939.

confinement with no mattress. After a few weeks at Armley I was transferred with more COs to Wakefield. I was handcuffed to a fellow prisoner who had been violent to a policeman, he had hung him up by his cape on a lamp-post. The deputy governor was a Quaker and whether he had a softer attitude to conchies I am not sure, but he asked me to black out the prison. But I was going to have no truck at all with ARP arrangements. It may sound extreme but that's how I felt about it and he didn't pursue the matter further. During 1941 and '42, the punishment cells of Wakefield Jail (where you got bread and water instead of the usual diet) were full of those who refused to do war work, this in some cases would be stitching blankets

to be used in the armed forces. I wasn't offered this work, but kept to stitching mailbags, but still got the same diet and the usual two or three days loss of remissionary sentence. I got this for refusing to take part in gas mask drill. I never wore a gas mask throughout the war.

When I came out I went freelancing in farm work all over the country until the authorities caught up with me. I had to go to the labour exchange and tell them what my position was and they said, 'You can get three months for that' and I said, 'I don't mind, I've just done nine'. So I carried on working and then I wrote to the Friends' mental hospital called the Retreat to ask if they wanted a porter, and they took me on. A great atmosphere of friendliness pervaded the Retreat. Everyone seemed to be trying to be nice to each other. Of course this suited me down to the ground. I did all sorts of jobs – cleaning windows, polishing floors, taking the post round, going into the wards emptying the rubbish. I was trying to make myself useful, willing to do anything. I was very happy indeed. They had a gramophone club and a bit of an orchestra which did the *Haydn Choral Symphony* and I played the part of the cuckoo on the recorder. I was fully expecting to be called up but I never was. So I received complete exemption from military service despite the verdict of the tribunal, but it was more luck than management. When the war ended they asked me to stop on at the Retreat and I became a hospital warden and spent nearly ten years there.

Ron Jeffrey, born 1915

CHAPTER 8
Leisure and entertainment

Cook, Troughton and Sims, Bishophill, York with Alan Ridsdill's grandfather, at the front, on the extreme left, 1900.

Alan Ridsdill at work at Cook, Troughton and Sims, as an instrument maker, 1959.

The Music Box Man

I started collecting when I was a small boy – stamps. I was absolutely fascinated, mainly by the early Victorian ones. I could picture where they'd been, on stage coaches and mail coaches, and some from across the seas. I'd spend all my pocket money on them. There was a little shop down Nunnery Lane which is no longer there, on the side nearest the city walls. There were rows of terraced houses and a little shop just before you got to the almshouses, which is a hotel now. They used to sell stamps.

Then I started collecting coins and I got fascinated with flintlock pistols. I remember looking in a shop in Petergate and there was a lovely eighteenth-century flintlock military pistol for £6 10s which was an awful lot of money and today would be several hundred pounds. I did save up and sold some of my coins and I started collecting pistols.

After I left school my father thought I ought to learn a trade, as his father and grandfather had, at Cooks, Troughton and Sims. So I was apprenticed as an optical instrument maker. Then I became interested in musical boxes. The first one I saw was when I was three, in the drawing-room of The Hermitage on Malton Road, it belonged to Wrights who had the famous shop selling the best pork pies in England. My uncle lived in the cottage and he was the stockman and my aunt used to clean inside the house and they took me in to see this box and it had dancing dolls on it. Years later

106

The Hermitage on Malton Road, once the home of the family of Wright's butcher's (where pigs were bred), 1930s.

Alan Ridsdill demonstrates a flintlock pistol in front of a group of boys at the Castle Museum, 1964.

Alan Ridsdill with his first Rolls Royce, in front of his workshop off Scarcroft Road, 1958.

Alan Ridsdill on top of the Castle Museum.

when I was on the staff at the Castle Museum, I'd got a collection of my own. Most of the boxes I had were broken because I couldn't afford the ones that were playing, but I had the machinery and the wherewithal to restore them. A gentleman came in and his mother had a musical box that didn't work. It had two dancing dolls and a nickel plated cylinder, one of the last boxes that were produced. They were competing with phonographs and gramophones by then. I said, 'Did this box used to be in the drawing room of the Hermitage before the war?' and he said, 'Yes'. I couldn't believe it, it was the first box I ever saw which eventually got me interested in musical boxes.

The first box I owned was in a photo album given by one of my grandmother's friends, Miss Shilling. It was a leather bound album full of

Victorian photographs. The first box I ever bought was a mandolin box by Bremonde made in Switzerland in the 1870s.

I was a founder member of the Musical Box Society of Britain and the meetings were nearly always in London. David Tallis, descendant of Thomas Tallis the composer was a member, and David Nixon the magician. I got my skills from Cooks, Troughton and Sims, my grandfather was apparently one of the best men at the firm, he used to build astronomical telescopes. I was in the fitting shop. I used to spend my summer holidays with an American chap who was a builder. He'd build a house, sell it and with the proceeds come over to England, hire a car and go round looking for clocks – double weighted Viennese regulators, Japanese stick clocks, quarter-striking skeleton clocks. Every clock has a different mechanism, the movement is the thing. Then I started with pianolas or player pianos. They were invented in the late nineteenth century and improved upon. It produces sixteen different degrees of touch, everything's on the pedalling, automatic from the rolls. And cars – my first was a Morris Minor which I bought in 1954 for £20 from the Inspector of Weights and Measures. Then I joined the Rolls Royce Enthusiast's Club.

I started it all at school, I worked at the Castle Museum even then, I used to do models and repair things at weekends. It's been unbelievable, I've made some really good friends.

Alan Ridsdill, born 1931

Dances and Suppers

I registered at the YWCA which was in Micklegate. It was a gentleman's residence at one time, at the corner of Micklegate and Barker Lane, double-fronted, and obviously stables at the back, walled gardens, very elegant and fine, the YW took great pride in it. And there were twenty-five women residents, and we had bed, breakfast, lunch, high tea, prayers and cocoa at nine, all for twenty-five shillings a week. I worked in the Civil Service, and that was two pound and fourpence. And you were considered very fortunate.

I used to go dancing a lot, a bit difficult in the YW, you had to be in for half past ten and lights out at eleven! So to get a key, she wanted to know where you were going and who with and she was really fed up with my friend and I always wanting to go dancing. She often said, 'When you two girls are as old as I am, you'll have bad hearts'. Later I got a very severe attack of flu and it laid me low. It was a really bad virus and I was off work for quite some time. A certificate went in and the doctor's writing was read as a 'dilapidated heart' when it was actually dilated! I never lived that down!

When I was courting, it was usually Friday we'd go to the Empire. He was in business and we usually went in the decent seats, then sometimes we had supper afterwards. I think he had a car, I met him in '32, and not every young man had a car! The Empire started at seven, we usually went to the first house, we didn't book or anything, there was no need, you queued up for the cheaper seats. I used to go to the De Grey Rooms very often on a Wednesday

109

night, they'd lovely dances there, and in Terry's restaurant in St Helen's Square. Beautiful restaurant, all mahogany and they had supper dances every month during the winter and it was two and six.

There were trips on the train from York to Scarborough, Sunday evening, that was two and six return, they were very popular. The spa was all evening dress, there were beautiful concerts and it all seemed very genteel. People looked nice and were well groomed and I think they behaved better. I do think dress and manners matter, they say it doesn't maketh a man, but I think it maketh them behave better.

Agnes Bridgewood, born 1908

The Bay Horse, Marygate

When we went in, in 1951, the landing was all dark brown varnished paper, gas brackets and gas lamps. And there used to be a board in the living room with loads of bells on. We'd no money, and I even cut a black velvet dance dress up to make a pelmet, and me brother made a bar. We put coconut matting on the floor and me brother helped to do it all up. It was a lovely bar, and it got real popular. When we got this little bar there were no pumps or 'owt like that, so I used to have me barrel of beer on a little gantry behind the bar and you had to bend down and give it seven and a half pulls to t' pint. Then we progressed and got a little hand pump so it was a bit easier and later on we got proper pumps.

We used to make lots of cocktails with sugar and all sorts. I was the first one to have a scarlet ceiling in me cocktail bar. I used to make drinks and flame 'em, set fire to 'em on winter nights. People used to be fascinated. You had your own gimmicks.

Twice we got flooded. We had a laugh though. We used to go in that big room then let the rope down with a basket. They used to come round with boats and put food in, and pull them up again. As soon as the floods come up, the first thing the council did was sandbags all the way up. You used to get all t' *Calendar* team [Yorkshire Television] standing there in their wellies. People still came in – on planks. On an afternoon all t' locals, from round about, used to go down to t' river and fish. All t' wives used to take it in turns to take a big tray of tea down.

We were one of the longest in Yorkshire, one of the longest in the same pub, as a tenant. Thirty-five years. But they were proper landlords and landladies in them days. You'd say 'good evening' and 'good night' if you see 'em go. Always. You've got to be the right sort of personality.

Eve Briggs, born 1919

Leeman Road Ferry

There was the ferry on Leeman Road, you paid a penny to go across to the Homestead. Just an ordinary boat, backwards and forwards. There was an ice rink at one time, back of Swinnerton Avenue, where they've built it all up. And there was a travelling fairground, same as they have on George's field but smaller scale. They used to come every year about

November time. We were a lot happier
than what they are today. You were
bathed every Saturday night in front of
the fire in an old tin bath and then on a
Sunday when you went to Sunday
school, you had a special dress on, all
white. You used to buy a new dress for
Easter or Whitsuntide, in them days,
and it was always white. And you had
white shoes and stockings on, always.

Ethel Smith, born 1909

Honesty Girls' Club

In the street where I live, [off Leeman
Road] there used to be an adult
school. The Honesty Girls' Club was
upstairs – they had a dance hall up some
steps and then there was a small place
off that to play cards and dominoes, and
in the bigger department was the
billiard hall, darts and a bar where you
could get soft drinks, crisps and
chocolate.

Gertie Hutchinson, born 1906

At The De Grey Rooms

I was married on the 9 April 1941 and
we opened the De Grey Rooms on the
12th, which was Easter Monday. Bert
died in '54, and I carried it on till '63, as
a restaurant and a dance hall; then
discos were coming in and that was not
my cup of tea, and I didn't renew my
lease. Bert was a great pianist, he had
his own band before we were married,
he played at the Folk Hall, New
Earswick in the 1930s with Frankie
Brown on drums, somebody called

Eve and Arthur Briggs dancing, 1950s.

Elliott on the trombone, and Bob
Halford, a policeman. They were mad
on waltzes, fox-trots and quicksteps.

We had wonderful staff. There was
quite a lot – the cloakrooms, the
restaurant, the chef, the kitchens. I
remember on one occasion, the Masonic
Lodge couldn't do this big affair. It was
the Marquis of Zetland, he was the
head. Bert was a mason and he said,
'Have the De Grey Rooms, with
pleasure'. So we got the staircase done
the day before, then I said, 'Do you
realise we've got a dance on till two
o'clock' and it had to be ready for nine
o'clock next morning. He said, 'You and
I will have to do it' but at one o'clock in
the morning all my staff turned up.
They'd heard that this function was on,

111

Bert Keech Band at De Grey Rooms. Bert is at the front, on the right, c. 1944.

Bert Keech band with girl singers at De Grey Rooms, 1944. Bert is the one nearest the girls.

and they came. For dancing, we used to get 300 in. And for a Saturday dance – by the Monday before the Saturday, we were sold out.

In the war, we had to have some fire watchers and Bert said if he paid for a firewatcher, he and I would count as the other two. It was frightening that night of the raid [1942]. A boulder from the Museum Gardens came on to the balcony of the De Grey Rooms. We were down in the bottom, in the grotto. After that night Bert said, 'We're going out' and we went out in the car, into the country. We shouldn't have done, but we did.

On VE night they were dancing in the square. It was absolutely wonderful, everybody behaved themselves, it was great. And Bert said to them, 'I've charged you all these years, everybody comes in free'.

We did weddings and luncheons for the rotary. It was hard going. Saturday we had to finish at twelve, but other nights we went on until two. We opened every night except Sunday. We used to get all the Air Vice Marshalls and officers. The Rotary used to meet every week at the De Grey Rooms for lunch, and the ladies luncheon club once a month, there was over 150 for the ladies, maybe 90 to 100 for the rotarians – and Bert was a rotarian as well. He was on the city council. The number of things he did for people – he was a Conservative councillor, but all the Labour men thought the world of him. He was on the Watch Committee and six policeman carried him at his funeral. And if he'd lived it was his turn to be Lord Mayor.

I really wonder now how I did it, because you didn't get to bed till about

VE Day at the De Grey Rooms, 1945.

The arches advertise York Pageant on Lendal Bridge, July 1909.

three and then I was up about seven o'clock. There were letters to see to and the phone. And I had my outfits to sort out. Hilda Anfield used to send me hats down when she got new ones in, she knew what kind I liked. They were in Blake Street, a lovely milliner's shop. Grisdales in Coney Street would send evening gowns round to see what I wanted. You had to look the part at the De Grey Rooms, you'd need a good wardrobe really. I've had a lovely life but I'd have had a better one with Bert.

Edith Keech, born 1913

Military Sunday

Of course Military Sunday was an event. They used to come out in full dress uniform and march down from the barracks through the market place, Coney Street to Duncombe Place and then to the Minster. The police were there and crowds would congregate along each side of the road in their hundreds. I got on the front line one day and I could hardly breathe, I was quite small at the time. We had the Royal Scots Greys and the First Royal Dragoons, they had very colourful uniforms, and there were infantry, chiefly West Yorkshire regiments. One interesting character who used to appear with the Scots Greys was Prince Arthur of Connaught.

George Thomas, born 1901

Four women in the Pageant, July 1909.

The Pageant

The pageant was in the Museum Gardens, right in front of Tempest Anderson Hall. People sat in the seats with their backs to the hall, and we saw them act from early Roman times, ancient Britons, and go right through the history of York. It was well worthwhile and it was surprising the number of people who were interested and took part.

George Thomas, born 1901

Mrs Jackman, a doctor's wife, had five sons who took part in the Pageant with her.

Amy Jackman, 1902.

Visit to County Hospital by the future King George and Queen Elizabeth, then Duke and Duchess of York, 1934.

In The Pageant

Canon Bell was the vicar of the church in Coney Street which was bombed during the war and he was wanting people to come and help with the pageant and I offered and took the children and he said, 'When you get the signal, rush forward with your children and shout', which I did. I was a peasant woman and the costume wasn't anything special. I had a long gown on and just ruffled. The children went with no shoes and no stockings and looked like they'd been running about all night. A lot of entertainment went on in those days, people made their own enjoyment. It changed when the gramophones came on the scene and the cinemas. For the museum gardens, we had to pay so much a year, and the governess used to take the children there in the afternoons and they'd run wild. Then they would come home and get a good wash. They were put in the bath together and whoever went in first had to come out first and there was always a little quarrel between them.

Amy Jackman, born 1884

Hospital Day

Hospital Day was a big occasion, and that's the only way they kept the hospitals open. It was one day in May and we had processions with carts through town, with the Salvation Army band in front and as you went along you collected money for the County Hospital; it was before the National Health. I'm going back to when Amy Johnson flew for the first time, and my dad decorated a bike as an aeroplane, put wings on it and I sat there with a flying cap. I'd got it from my cousin that was in the Air Force. I won first prize.

Eileen Potter, born 1919

Mad About The Theatre

At York Theatre Royal, in 1935 it became the York Repertory Company and the rep were twice nightly in those days. I don't know how they got anybody to do it – to change the programme each week. Fourpence in the gallery, sevenpence in the upper circle, ninepence in the pit, one and six in the stalls and two and six in the dress circle.

The wartime programmes, some of them were single sheets, because of the paper drive. In wartime there was the closing of the theatres in London and for a time that meant more touring. I remember being in the theatre on VE night, everything was happening outside

The Buffs, Monkgate. The tallest man, at the back, is Mr Hardisty.

and we were inside. My diary for Wednesday 9 May 1945 says, 'Day off. Went to *Noah* at the theatre. Went out at 11 p.m. to see lights, fireworks and celebrations'.

Marjorie Leng, born 1923

The 'Buffs'

I lived at the Bay Horse in Blossom Street. Clubs used to meet there. There was the 'Royal Antideluvian Order of Buffaloes' and I imagine they were a friendly society of some sort but they were very secretive. They used to wear regalia similar to the Masons with a decoration round the neck and names of the Grand Masters inscribed on little plates on it. They had medals, and ornamental cuffs which reached nearly up to their elbows, and a very ornate apron with gold braiding, or it was more likely to be some sort of composition of brass hanging down in fringes. The inaugural meeting was to take place on the 11 November 1918, and because of that – quite without authority – my grandfather said, 'This will be known as the Scarcroft Victory Lodge'.

The Buffs had various officers, and the door into the clubroom had cut a little trap door about six inches square, and I was told that the official in charge of that was known as the 'City Tiler' and that anyone that knocked, he opened this door, looked through, and if he recognised a brother, he was admitted. This was the routine, no-one could come into the room without being recognised. There was a password and I heard that new members had to show that they had courage.

I did hear that the Buffaloes had been meeting in the Lowther after the war. And my grandfather was the Grand Master, just as he'd been the chairman of the original York Cricket Club, and chairman of the York Swimming Club. I think my grandfather was chairman of practically everything that was on the go in York at that time!

Ron Powell, born 1921

CHAPTER 9

All kinds of transport

Boat trip on *Summer Breeze* on the River Ouse. The man at the front is Bert Keech.

The River King

I remember sitting on my grandfather's shoulder, he was stood on Ouse Bridge, looking down to where the little boats were. There was a steam boat, I think it was the *River King* illuminated with all lights. There was a band on board playing patriotic music, and that was 1905 which was the centenary of the battle of Trafalgar.

George Thomas, born 1901

The Pony and Trap

I can remember going to friends at Cottingwith and father used to hire a pony and trap. You could hire them by

The *River King*, 1930.

Lendal Bridge, down at the bottom was a horse repository. Sometimes it would be a governess cart where three of us sat in, and sometimes it was a dogcart with two at the back and I didn't like that, I always felt I was going to fall out. I can see us now going clop clop clop down Fulford Road. Fortunately the friends we went to, he was a farmer, and he used to take the horse out of the trap and put it in the stable and harness it. I'm sure we'd never have got home, the horse would have gone off without us if my father had harnessed it. He could drive it and that was about all.

Maude Worfolk, born 1910

Wednesday Treat

It was a treat on a Wednesday afternoon when mother met me from school. We used to go on the tram from Blossom Street to Haxby Road, the terminus was just before you went over the hill. On the top of the tram, they'd take the trolley pole, swing it round and put it back on the top and then you could turn the seats, they were only wooden. If you were lucky and got the front seat, it was lovely. When we got older when Rowntrees Park was built, we could play tennis and paddle. Sixpence an hour each for tennis and then – luxury of luxuries – you went to the café and you had an ice cream or a fruit drink. Lime juice was my favourite.

Maude Worfolk, born 1910

The First Aeroplanes

In 1911 a great event took place, when the first aeroplanes arrived in York onto

City walls. A tram travels over Lendal Bridge, *c.* 1910.

the Knavesmire. They were there for a few days and we could go and have a look. There was no radio in those days but they made quite a fuss in the local newspaper. In 1913 the Yorkshire Show was held in York, on Knavesmire, the one that is held at Harrogate today. One of the things was the aeroplanes again. The *Daily Mail* got into the act and in September 1913, in between the visit of the Royal Flying Corps, the *Daily Mail* came up with this aeroplane. You could pay, I think it was a pound, and have a flight round York.

George Thomas, born 1901

Motorbiking

My father bought a motorbike, it was an AJS, rather a heavy machine. I should be about fourteen and I used to start it up and take it round to the front for them, and often take my friend for a ride, there were no laws to say that you couldn't. We had a Peace Day the year after the war finished, 1919, and we decided to go off for the day on the motorbike, my mother in the sidecar and me sitting on the carrier at the back. My father didn't know anything about driving and when he had been on a bicycle he used to go in top gear, and so we came down Garrowby Hill in top gear and it gathered up speed until something was in the road and it turned his wheel and the whole cycle shot into the side and heaved us all off and I seemed to go down a sort of hole. But there were none of us hurt. Everybody was out celebrating Peace Sunday and do you know we couldn't get any help at all so we had to leave the bike and walk home from Garrowby Hill [about twelve miles] and on the way home there was a man sitting at his gate, and he was a grumpy old thing, and we were so

M. Salmet, the 'Daily Mail aviator', visits York in September 1913.

The AJS motorbike in the 1930s. Maurice James is pictured with a friend.

desperate that we took more or less no notice of him and we went into his house and made ourselves a cup of tea and proceeded to walk for the rest of it.

Hilda Beaumont, born 1904

A Hot Air Balloon

The Gala at Bootham Park was a most interesting affair and they had it every year. There was the man with a captive balloon which stayed up for a time and came down and that was for everyone who'd like to pay to go up. So I went up in the balloon and enjoyed it very much, went right up and sat in the basket for a long time looking all around.

Amy Jackman, born 1884

Running Up That Hill

The first motorbike and sidecar we had, the sidecar was like a basket chair and had a foot rest. Mother used to sit in it and I sat between her knees on a stool with a rug wrapped round to hold me in. She used to make bonnets out of felt with chiffon veils and I had one as well because there were no windscreens and the roads were frightfully dusty, they were like farm roads. My father wore his cap back to front and he had some old overalls which at one time had been waterproof but they'd lost their waterproof feeling.

It had a belt drive, not a chain, to drive it and it just used to whizz round when it was wet and didn't drive. During the First World War, petrol was scarce. Being an engineer, father adapted the bike and he used to carry a medicine bottle of petrol to put into the carburettor to start it, then switch over to paraffin! Then we got one with a windscreen and I went onto the pillion seat and I was one of the first pillion riders in York. It wasn't padded like they are now, it was a piece of iron and dipped down in the centre with six springs, and you sat sideways, you didn't straddle. My father was 'a bit of a driver' and mother and I had to go over onto the sidecar when he turned a corner or else you went up the bank. When you went to Whitby, you made your will before you left!

In the early days with the first motorbike, mother and I used to walk up Whitwell Hill and he used to run beside the bike with the engine going to get it up. The last motorbike we had was an eight horsepower AJS and that was what he loved to go solo.

Maude Worfolk, born 1910

Amy Jackman's certificate of ascent in a balloon at York Gala, 1912.

Northern Motor Utilities

We lived in Dundee Street adjoining the NMU garage, in a company house, rented from NMU. My dad was a tinsmith there. It was quite a sight on an evening because NMU used to service the Rowntrees' vans, which were brown with 'Rowntrees' in cream on the side, and they'd queue up to come into the garage around half past four. It can't have been very healthy with those obnoxious fumes in a small street. The garage was at the bottom of the street and Mrs Levitt, one of our neighbours, ran the canteen at the top. At lunchtime there was the loud sound of hobnail boots as the workmen ran to be

Maude Worfolk with her mother, on a motorbike in 1924.

first in the queue. My father would have been using flux as part of the soldering process, and when he came home from work you could still smell the flux. We would have a 'mad half hour' when we'd wrestle about on the floor. Even now when I smell flux, I'm reminded of those happy days.

Mike Race, born 1938

Cars After The War

My first car was an air-cooled Rover tourer, one stroke engine, disc wheels, high pressure tyres, oh it was a rough ride. It kicked like a donkey. We went on holiday to Wales and I had to look at the engine once or twice and the magneto magnet was coming off so I got the hammer shaft and banged it down, and off we went again. Then I had a Jowett two-seater, nice little car, bit rough but it

was all right. The first journey was to Morecambe to a planning weekend and coming back a gasket went, and I got stuck between Skipton and Settle on Monday morning. Then I had a Wolseley coupé, six cylinder, that was a nice job. I had a Baby Austin through the war, ran around in that, then I had one of those Morris 10s. For a month or two I had a Riley but I took that back to the firm, then I bought my first new one, the Singer 10, wasn't a bad job at all. Then I had one of the new Fords that came out, with a rounded front and the gear change on the steering wheel, then a Ford 10. Then I bought a second-hand Princess Van den Plas, that was a beautiful car but it went so rusty that it went to almost nothing and cost hundreds of pounds to put right. Then I got a Mazda, they're reliable, no trouble. I have taxis now, it's a lot cheaper than any motor car, I can tell you.

Charles Minter, born 1897

Northern Motor Utilities, Walmgate Bar, 1928.

124

CHAPTER 10

Century of change

Micklegate Bar and Blossom Street, 1925.

Nell McTurk (née Wildon), c. 1916.

Nell McTurk was born in March 1896 and her great-grandson Toby Wilson was born ninety-one years later in April 1987. Between them is a century of change. Nell was the youngest of thirteen children, two of whom died in infancy. She was born at home, and her mother died when she was a year old, worn out with giving birth and living in dire circumstances, so Nell was brought up by her eldest sister. Toby was born in hospital, the youngest of two children, and both parents are still alive.

Nell left school at the age of twelve and went into service. Her family could not afford to send her on to further education. Toby, now aged twelve, is in his second year at secondary school and plans to go to sixth form college and university. When

Nell was born, women were still a long way off from having the vote. When Toby was born, the first female British prime minister had been in power for eight years.

Toby's family own a semi-detached house, where he has his own room and television, and he receives weekly pocket money. Nell's family rented a small terraced house and she shared a bedroom with her sisters. She didn't get pocket money but recalls,

I used to run miles on errands for people for a bit of cake or a bun. My dad used to play pop 'cos I was always wearing my boots out. He had a last and I'd go for some leather for him, it was in a big basket, a piece of boot leather for fivepence. If we got a ha'penny, we thought the world of it. And if you had an apple, they were all round you wanting a bite, and they'd wait to get the core. We always ate orange peel, we wouldn't waste a bit of it. At Christmas we got an apple, an orange and a penny and maybe a little toy doll from the Penny Bazaar and then you'd ask for a bit of rag to make some clothes for it. And I was really grateful.

In 1900, there were 37 million people living in Britain, 87% of whom lived in towns. 75,000 people lived in York. As we approach the year 2000, the national population has increased to nearly 59 million, with York's population at 176,000.

The nineteenth century was a period of great inventions – the railway, police force, bicycles, photography, postage stamps, electric light, trams, efficient sewerage systems, the telephone, rubber tyres and the car. The twentieth century is the age of technology – the aeroplane, moving pictures, the space rocket, man on the Moon, hi-fi music centres, the computer and the mobile telephone.

In 1900 cars were owned by the rich, and had to keep to a speed limit of 14mph. The first car to be registered in York was in the year 1904. In 2000 most households in Britain have at least one car, and although the speed limit is 70mph, cars are capable of travelling at 100mph or more.

In 1900, 80% of the population were working class, ruled over by the other 20%. There was no National Health Service, no national insurance and a poor education system. The First World War, however, was to effect many changes.

Nell went to Fishergate school where she enjoyed reading, writing and arithmetic. She used a slate and chalk in the classroom. Toby's school has 1,200 pupils. He studies 15 subjects which include arts and sciences, design and technology, textiles, and personal and social health education. He uses a rollerball pen to write in exercise books, but also works on a computer. If Toby misbehaved at school, he would get lines, have to stay in at break time or get a detention. In 1900 children were caned for quite small misdemeanours.

Nell recalls her leisure activities,

We used to go and slide down into the cattle pens off the bar walls. We liked skipping and running races. At home we played ludo and snakes and ladders, played with four or five checks, a ball or skipping rope. If you'd a gramophone it was something, but sometimes it was cracked and there was a song that kept going, 'Mickey Dooley' over and over.

Toby spends his leisure time,

Cycling, playing football, games on the computer, going to town with friends, swimming, roller blading, skateboarding, youth clubs, juggling club, the cinema, tenpin bowling and to cafés.

Most of these activities were unheard of in 1900. Even the food he likes was not available at that time:

Toby Wilson, 1999.

Croissants, burgers, pizzas, baguettes, doughnuts and hot dogs.

But he thinks they ate better in the past,

Really healthy foods, a lot of meat and fish, and apples.

Nell explains that food was not so easy to obtain,

If my dad had a boiled egg, we used to take it in turns having the top of it. You'd think it was something wonderful. You never had an egg, except at Easter and then we'd hard boil it, colour it and roll it down the hill on Low Moor while it broke. Then we'd eat it. We used to go to the market before they closed at eight o'clock on a Saturday night, there were no fridges to keep things in. They had to sell everything off. And the Shambles was all butcher's shops and I'd go and beat 'em down for a piece of best end of brisket boned. They said a shilling and I shouted, 'I'll have it'. A big joint, it did for nine of us.

Toby identifies the items, commonplace in his life, which would not have been present in 1900,

Freezers, washing machines and driers, showers and double glazing, computers, televisions, CD players, electric guitars, central heating, football boots and trainers, video cameras and video recorders. We have modern technology and we have more money.

He decides that he wouldn't have liked to live a century ago because,

Life was harder then. They might go to the park and think that is a good holiday. A holiday to us is going to the other side of the world.

Toby believes that nowadays we have more access to knowledge.

There's libraries and computers. The Internet gives you access to the whole world. Instead of using the phone, you've got your own e-mail code and you can talk to your uncle in Australia. You've got the world at your fingertips.

At the end of the twentieth century, York is a place hardly recognisable by our ancestors. They would have walked through the cobbled streets, only the better off amongst them being able to afford a penny for a ride on a horse tram. Toby explains,

In 1900 they never dreamed of Neil Armstrong walking on the moon, but he did in 1969, the first man to step on a different planet. Cool! In the future they might get to Jupiter or even discover a new galaxy. People might start living on the moon and build houses there. They've discovered a liquid there and they don't know if it's water. They might have hovercraft cars and faster ways to travel. There'll be pocket televisions or pocket bikes which you get out and press a special button. Things are getting smaller and smaller apart from us, we are expanding the population.